Conquering First Grade

Reading
Mathematics
Science
Social Studies
Writing

Jodene Lynn Smith, M.A.

Publishing Credits

Corinne Burton, M.A.Ed., *President*; Conni Medina, M.A.Ed., *Managing Editor*; Emily R. Smith, M.A.Ed., *Content Director*; Lynette Ordoñez, *Editor*; Evan Ferrell, *Graphic Designer*; Lubabah Memon, *Assistant Editor*

Image Credits

pp. 52, 97 Illustrations by Timothy J. Bradley; all other images from iStock and/or Shutterstock.

Standards

Shell Education
A division of Teacher Created Materials
5301 Oceanus Drive
Huntington Beach, CA 92649-1030
www.tcmpub.com/shell-education
ISBN 978-1-4258-1620-9

Table of Contents

Dear Family,

Welcome to *Conquering First Grade*. First grade will be an exciting and challenging year for your child. This book is designed to supplement the concepts your child is learning in first grade and to strengthen the connection between home and school. The activities in this book are based on today's standards and provide practice in reading, word study, language, writing, mathematics, social studies, and science. It also features fun, yet challenging, critical-thinking activities and games. In addition to the activity sheets in this book, the end of each section also provides engaging extension activities.

Your child should complete one unit per month, including the extension activities. This will allow your child to think about grade-level concepts over a longer period of time. This also ensures that the book can be completed in one school year.

Keep these tips in mind as you work with your child this year:

- Set aside specific times each week to work on the activities.
- Have your child complete one or two activities each time, rather than an entire unit at one time.
- Keep all practice sessions with your child positive and constructive. If the mood becomes tense or you and your child get frustrated, set the book aside and find another time to practice.
- Help your child with instructions, if necessary. If your child is having difficulty understanding what to do, work through some of the problems together.
- Encourage your child to do his or her best work, and compliment the effort that goes into learning.

Enjoy the time learning with your child during first grade. Summer will be here before you know it!

Sincerely,

The Shell Education Staff

Suggested Family Activities

You can extend your child's learning by taking fun family field trips. A wide variety of experiences helps expand and develop a child's vocabulary. Field trips also provide greater context and meaning to his or her learning in school.

A Trip to a Museum

Your first stop should be the gift shop. Have your child pick five postcards of artifacts or paintings in the museum. Then, as you visit the museum, your child should be on the lookout for the five items he or she chose. It's an individual scavenger hunt! If he or she finds all five, you can celebrate the accomplishment!

A Trip to a National Park

The National Park Service has a great program called Junior Rangers. If you go to a local park, check in with the rangers at the visitors center to see what tasks your child can complete to earn a Junior Ranger patch and/or certificate. Your child can also go to the WebRangers site (www.nps.gov/webrangers/) and check out a vacation spot, play games, and earn virtual rewards!

A Trip to a Zoo

Before your trip, create a Zoo Bingo card. Include various characteristics that your child should look for (for example, a warm-blooded animal, an animal with feathers, an animal from Africa, etc.). Bring the Zoo Bingo card and a small clipboard with you. Have your child write or draw the name of one animal that fits each category. An animal should only be used for one category/box. When he or she gets bingo, celebrate the accomplishment!

A Trip to a Library

Help your child discover new books. First, ask your child what his or her favorite type of story is. For example: *Do you like funny stories or adventure stories better?* Choose three books that fit the topic or interest that your child selected. Read the story aloud with your child. As you read, ask your child to explain how the pictures match the text.

A Trip to a Farmers' Market

Farmers' markets are great places to learn about different fruits and vegetables. Ask your child to help you find the colors of the rainbow. At each fruit or vegetable stand, ask your child to locate one color from the rainbow. Then, explain what the fruit or vegetable is and the different types of recipes it can be used in. For example, a red tomato can be used for ketchup, pizza, pasta sauce, etc.

Suggested Family Activities *(cont.)*

By discussing the activities in this book, you can enhance your child's learning. But it doesn't have to stop there. The suggestions below provide even more ideas on how to support your child's education.

General Skills

- Make sure your child gets plenty of exercise. Children need about 60 minutes of physical activity each day. You may want to have your child sign up for a sport. Or you can do fun things as a family, such as swimming, riding bicycles, or hiking.
- It's also important for children to get plenty of sleep. Children this age need between 9–11 hours of sleep each night. Establish a nightly bedtime routine that involves relaxing activities such as a warm shower or bath or reading a story.

Reading Skills

- Help build your child's comprehension skills by asking questions about what they've read. For example, you could ask why he or she thinks a character has done something, or you could ask what he or she thinks will happen next.
- Encourage your child to reread his or her favorite books, stories, or poems. Rereading will help your child read more quickly and accurately.

Writing Skills

- Have your child keep a daily diary/journal about activities he or she is doing during time off from school. He or she can draw pictures or write words or sentences.
- Ask your child to help you write in everyday situations. You can have him or her help you write a grocery list or write a thank-you note.

Mathematics Skills

- Ask your child to compare different objects' sizes. For example, have your child put his or her toys in order from biggest to smallest or ask your child which of two objects is smaller or bigger, etc.
- Encourage your child to practice telling time. If you are going to a movie, a special event, or even an appointment, ask your child to help you figure out what time you should leave. For example: *If the movie begins at 3:30 p.m. and it takes 15 minutes to get there, what time should we leave?* Be sure to point to the clock hands to support your child.

Directions: Read the text, and answer the questions.

A New Pet

Mom said I can buy a pet! She said a mouse is fun. A mouse likes to play. It does not take a lot of work. I read a book about mice. I must get mouse food. I can get it at the pet store. My mouse will need water, too. It will be fun to have a mouse.

1. Who tells the child she can buy a pet?
   - (A) the girl
   - (B) the mouse
   - (C) Mom

2. What kind of pet is a mouse?
   - (A) bad
   - (B) fun
   - (C) fast

3. Where can the child get mouse food?
   - (A) at home
   - (B) at the pet store
   - (C) at a farm

4. What is a mouse?
   - (A) a toy
   - (B) a color
   - (C) an animal

Directions: Read the text, and answer the questions.

Apples

Apples are good to eat. Have you seen an apple tree? You can pick apples in the fall. That is when they are ripe. Cut an apple in two. The middle is called the *core*. Look at a seed. A big tree can grow from that little seed!

1. Where do apples grow?
   - (A) on a bush
   - (B) on a tree
   - (C) on a farm

2. When can you best pick apples?
   - (A) in the fall
   - (B) in the summer
   - (C) in the spring

3. What does the word *ripe* mean?
   - (A) red
   - (B) older
   - (C) ready

4. What is the middle of an apple called?
   - (A) a stem
   - (B) a seed
   - (C) a core

Directions: Write the word from the Word Bank that matches the clue.

Word Bank

- with
- they
- are
- from
- have

1. This word has the short *i* sound.

2. This word begins with *th*.

3. This word rhymes with *come*.

4. The third letter in this word is *v*.

5. This word rhymes with *car*.

Directions: Answer each question.

1. Write the word that needs a capital letter.

   My friend sam is funny.

2. Complete the sentence with a name.

   My friend ________________ is nice.

3. Rewrite the sentence using correct capitalization.

   dr. kim checks teeth.

4. Write today's date using a capital letter.

5. Write the word that needs a capital letter.

   My dog's name is spot.

Directions: Write the name of an animal you like in each circle. Color the circle with your favorite animal. Then, write two reasons why you like this animal.

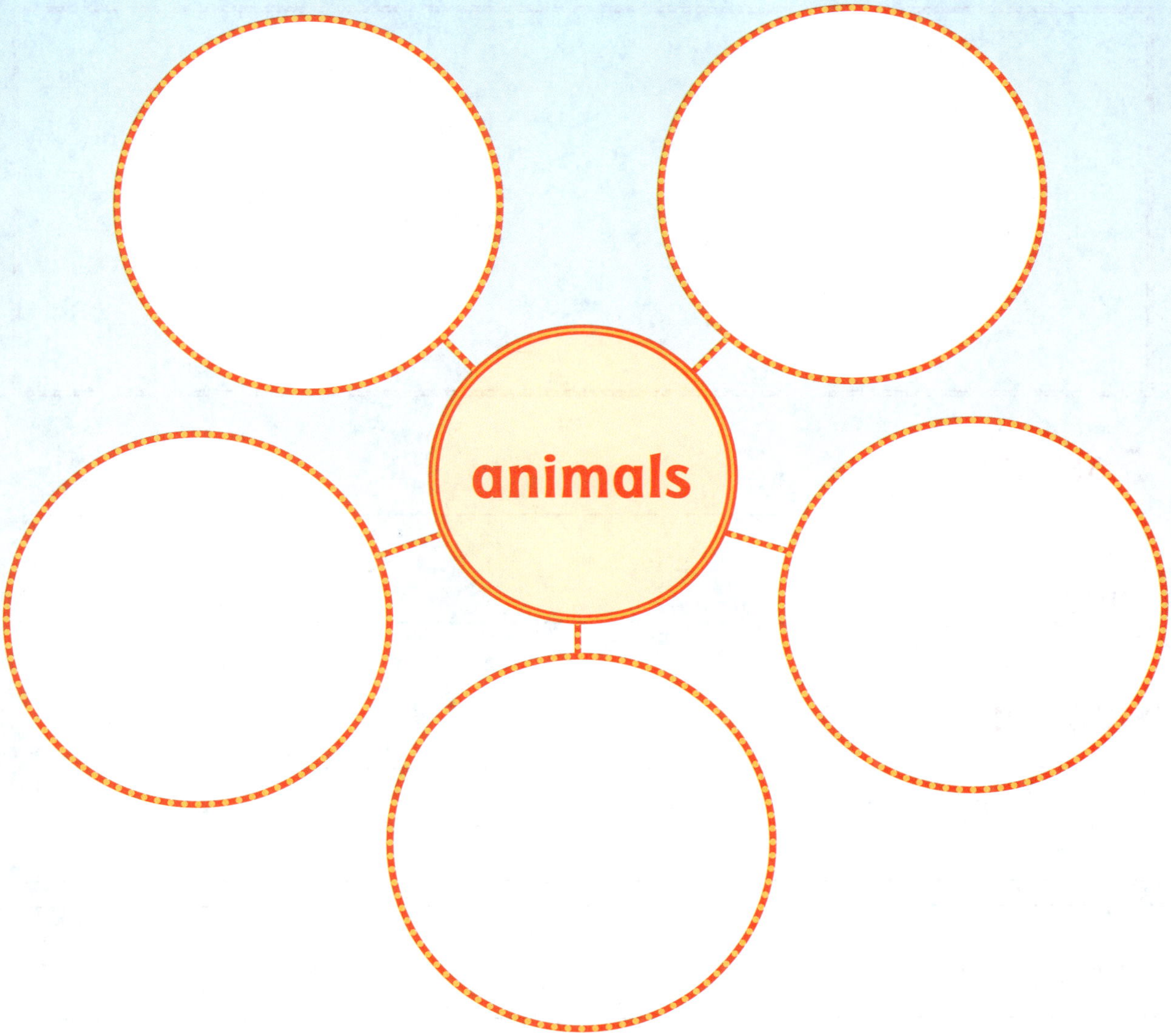

Reason 1

____

Reason 2

____

UNIT 1

Writing

Directions: Draw and write about your favorite animal. Include reasons why you like it. Use your notes from page 11 to help you. Then, fill in the checklist.

Opinion

I like ________________________________.

Reasons

____

____

Checklist

- [ ] Sentences begin with capital letters.
- [ ] Sentences end with punctuation.
- [ ] There are spaces between the words.

Directions: Solve each problem.

1 How many in all? ____

2 How many in all? ____

3 How many in all? ____

4 How many in all? ____

5 Add. ____

6 Add. ____

Directions: Solve each problem.

1. 37 has ________ tens and ________ ones.

2. Write the numeral.

____

3. Write the number that has 4 ones and 2 tens.

____

4. What is the largest number that can be made with 1 and 8?

____

5. What is the smallest number that can be made with 6 and 1?

____

6. Draw tens rods and ones cubes to show the number 12.

Directions: Add to the picture. Solve the problem.

Lee is making cupcakes for her birthday party. She puts 12 cupcakes on a tray. Then, she adds 6 more. How many cupcakes does Lee have now?

____

__________ cupcakes

Directions: Read and solve the problem.

Problem: Connor is counting his toy cars. He counts 10 toy cars. Then, he counts 7 more. How many toy cars does Connor have now?

What Do You Know?	What Is Your Plan?
Draw a picture to solve the problem.	How will you count?

Solve the Problem!

____

______________________ toy cars

Directions: Maps use drawings called symbols to show where things are. Draw a symbol you can use for each map location.

street	school
park	bank
river	house

Directions: Follow the steps in this experiment to track when the sun rises.

What You Need

newspaper weather sections or online weather reports for five days in a row

	Sunrise	Sunset
Day 1		
Day 2		
Day 3		
Day 4		
Day 5		

What to Do

1. Each day, look at the weather section to find when the sun rises and sets. Add the data to the chart.
2. What season is it?
3. What do you notice about the sunrise times?
4. What do you notice about the sunset times?

Think About It!

Will the times be the same during other seasons? How can you find out?

Directions: Use the code to find the answer to the joke.

Code:
Write the letter that comes after the one written.

Example:

d	o	g
c	n	f

___ ___ ___   ___ ___ ___ ___ ___
R g d   j d d o r

___ ___ ___ ___ ___ ___ ___
q t m m h m f

___ ___ ___ ___   ___ ___ ___ ___
z v z x   e q n l

___ ___ ___   ___ ___ ___ ___ !
s g d   a z k k

Directions: Find the value of each word. Use the example to help you.

A = 1 ten	I = 3 tens	U = 5 tens
E = 2 tens	O = 4 tens	Any Consonant = 1 one

Word	Equation	Total
1 with	1 + 30 + 1 + 1 =	33
2 they		
3 are		
4 from		
5 have		

6 Which word has the greatest value?

____

7 Write a word that has a value over 75.

____

High-Frequency Words Activity

Make a list of the high-frequency words from page 9. Look through the pages of your favorite book. Add a tally mark to your list each time you see one of the words in your book.

Writing Activity

Reread your writing on page 12. Circle the first word of each sentence. Make sure it begins with a capital letter.

Mathematics Activity

Write the age of each person who lives in your house. Then, write or draw how many tens and how many ones are in each number you wrote.

Social Studies Activity

Look at a map of where you live. Find the key. Name each symbol in the key, and then find it on the map. Compare the symbols you drew on page 17. Were any the same as the symbols on the map?

Critical-Thinking Activity

Use the code from page 19 to write a secret message. Give the message and the code to someone. See if he or she can decode your message.

Listening-and-Speaking Activity

Tell the joke from page 19 to someone else. Make sure you ask the question and then wait for them to respond before you tell the punch line.

Directions: Read the text, and answer the questions.

The Parade

Mark and Pam love to dress up. "We should have a parade!" says Mark.

Mark and Pam ask Kim and Lee to help. They bring their dogs along.

Mark says, "We can have a pet parade instead!"

Lee puts a cowboy hat on his dog. Kim dresses her dog in a clown hat and skirt. Pam puts bunny ears on her cat. Mark puts his cat in a stroller. The parade is a lot of fun!

1. What do Mark and Pam love to do?
   - (A) go on hikes
   - (B) dress up
   - (C) take naps

2. Who helps Mark and Pam?
   - (A) the dogs
   - (B) Kim and Lee
   - (C) the pets

3. Who gets dressed up?
   - (A) Lee
   - (B) the pets
   - (C) Pam

4. Which pet is dressed like a rabbit?
   - (A) Lee's dog
   - (B) Kim's dog
   - (C) Pam's cat

Directions: Read the text, and answer the questions.

Busy Working

Ants have different jobs. Ants have a queen just like bees do. The queen's job is to lay the eggs. All the other ants work for her. Some worker ants look for food. They use a scent to mark a trail to the food. Then, more ants can find the food. Have you had an ant bite? Some ants will bite or sting to stay safe. Most ants just want to do their jobs.

1. How are ants and bees alike?
   - (A) They both like honey.
   - (B) They live in the same place.
   - (C) They both have a queen.

2. What does the queen do?
   - (A) She makes the ants work.
   - (B) She lays the eggs.
   - (C) She gets the food.

3. A worker ant finds food. What happens next?
   - (A) The ants use a scent to mark a trail.
   - (B) More ants look for food.
   - (C) Ants stay in the nest.

4. Why do some ants bite?
   - (A) to get food
   - (B) to get to the nest
   - (C) to stay safe

Directions: Write each word from the Word Bank in the correct column. A word may appear in more than one column.

Word Bank

- for
- that
- was
- were
- what
- how

Words that begin with *w*	Words that have the letter *a*	Words that have three letters

Directions: Add ending punctuation.

1. Where are we going _____
2. I am very excited for the sleepover _____
3. Where is my lunch _____
4. The bus stopped _____
5. What time is it _____
6. Watch out _____
7. Today was a good day _____
8. The book is on the desk _____

Directions: Write a question.

Directions: Think about a time you played with a friend. Complete the chart with notes about the day. Then, draw pictures of two events from the day.

Who?	
Where?	
When?	

Event 1

Event 2

Directions: Draw and write about a time you played with a friend. Use your ideas from page 26 to help you. Then, fill in the checklist.

Checklist

- ☐ Sentences begin with capital letters.
- ☐ Sentences end with punctuation.
- ☐ There are spaces between the words.

Directions: Solve each problem.

1. How many in all?

______

2. Four are crossed off. How many are left?

______

3. Subtract. Cross off two. How many are left?

6 – 2 = ______

4. Subtract. Cross off five. How many are left?

5 – 5 = ______

5. Subtract.

______ – ______ = ______

Directions: Solve each problem.

1. Name the smaller shapes that compose the rectangle.

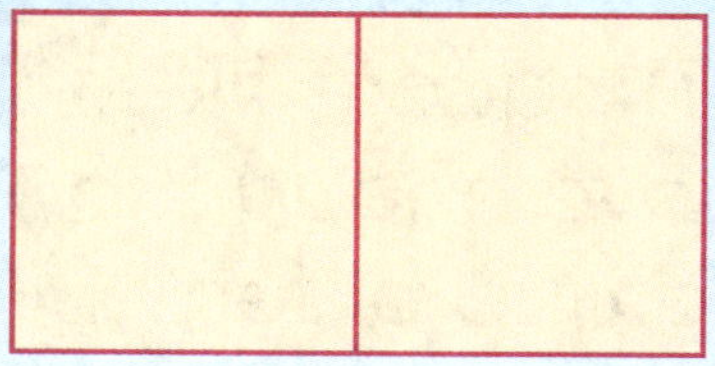

2. Name the smaller shapes that compose the square.

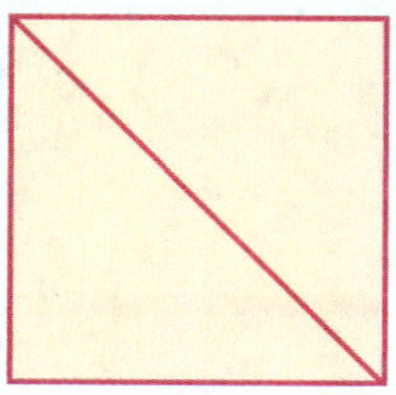

3. Name the larger shape that is composed of the trapezoids.

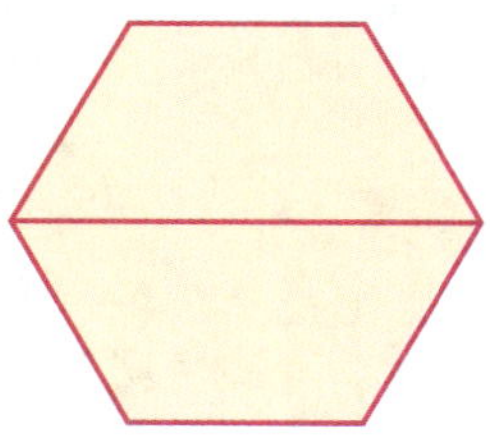

4. Name the larger shape that is composed of the triangles.

UNIT 2

Problem Solving

Directions: Draw a picture to solve the problem.

_____ group of ten with _____ left over

Directions: Read and solve the problem.

Problem: Mr. King's class got 14 new books. He stacks the books in groups of ten. How many groups of ten will he make? Are there any books left over?

What Do You Know?

How many books are there?

__________ books

What Is Your Plan?

How can you make groups of ten?

Solve the Problem!

__________ ten and __________ ones

Directions: Draw a tool each community worker needs to do his or her job.

Community Worker	Tool

Directions: Follow the steps in this experiment to discover how plants are different.

What You Need

- plastic hoop
- notebook

What to Do

1. Take a plastic hoop to an area with a lot of plants.
2. Place your hoop flat on the grass.
3. Study the plants inside your plastic hoop. In your notebook, draw or describe each plant.
4. Count the number of each type of plant inside the hoop. Write the number of each plant next to its drawing.
5. Move the hoop to a different area, and compare the results. Are there different plants in this new area? How do you know?

Directions: Write two more words for each category.

Things That Can Fly	Animals That Jump
bird	frog
airplane	kangaroo

Directions: Write the name of each category.

calf	tuba
puppy	drums
kitten	flute
lamb	violin

Directions: Play a category game. Write words that begin with the letters in each category. Challenge yourself by setting a timer. Try to finish in under two minutes.

Plants/Flowers	Shapes
c ______	c ______
d ______	d ______
r ______	r ______
s ______	s ______
t ______	t ______

High-Frequency Words Activity

Pick a piece of writing you've done this month. Circle any high-frequency words from page 24. If you did not use any of the words, figure out a place you can use some of them.

Language Activity

Think of a hand motion for each type of ending punctuation mark. Have someone read sentences to you. Use your hand motions to show which type of ending punctuation should go at the end of each sentence.

Mathematics Activity

Work with blocks to compose shapes. Figure out what shapes you can use to make larger squares and rectangles.

Social Studies Activity

Look around town for community workers as you are going places. Talk about the workers you see, the jobs they do, and the tools they use.

Science Activity

Plant a seed in your yard, a cup, or a pot. Watch the seed grow. Name the parts of the plant as they grow.

Listening-and-Speaking Activity

Play a game with someone. Pick a category. Take turns naming a word in the category that begins with each letter of the alphabet from A to Z.

Directions: Read the text, and answer the questions.

Earning Money

Jin wants to make some money.

Mom says, "I have two jobs you can do. You can rake the leaves. Then, you can dig up the garden."

Jin rakes the leaves and digs up the garden. He wants to work some more.

Mom says, "You can take out the trash now." Mom tells Jin there is one big chore to do. "You need to clean your bedroom."

Jin asks, "Do I have to?"

1. Why does Jin need a job?
   - (A) Jin wants some money.
   - (B) Jin likes to work.
   - (C) Mom wants Jin to work.

2. Where does Jin work first?
   - (A) in the garden
   - (B) in the house
   - (C) at school

3. What jobs does Jin do?
   - (A) He rakes and mows the yard.
   - (B) He rakes and sweeps the leaves.
   - (C) He rakes the leaves and digs up the garden.

4. Which job does Jin **not** want to do?
   - (A) take out the trash
   - (B) clean his bedroom
   - (C) rake the leaves

Directions: Read the text, and answer the questions.

Teeth

Animals use teeth to help them eat. Teeth can be sharp or flat.

A wolf has sharp teeth to eat meat. Wolf teeth are shaped to help it rip and tear. Animals that eat meat are called *carnivores*.

Cows do not eat meat. They do not need sharp teeth to rip and tear. They eat grass. Most cow teeth are flat for chewing. Animals that do not eat meat are called *herbivores*.

1. What word tells about wolf teeth?
   - Ⓐ flat
   - Ⓑ sharp
   - Ⓒ square

2. What do wolves eat?
   - Ⓐ meat
   - Ⓑ trees
   - Ⓒ grass

3. Why do cows not have sharp teeth?
   - Ⓐ They do not need to tear meat.
   - Ⓑ They chew bones and grass.
   - Ⓒ They wear them down by chewing meat.

4. What do cows eat?
   - Ⓐ bones
   - Ⓑ meat
   - Ⓒ grass

Directions: Write the word that fits in each word shape.

Word Bank

- two
- some
- about
- said
- use
- there

1

2

3

4

5

6

Directions: Answer each question.

1. Circle the noun.

   The bird flew away.

2. Circle the nouns.

   The chair is beside the desk.

3. Write the noun.

   The ______________ zoomed by.
   (small or bee)

4. Write the noun.

   The ______________ growls.
   (tiger or green)

5. Write the noun.

   Her ______________ is blue.
   (dress or pretty)

Directions: Think about your country's flag. Read the ideas in the web. Then, add three more ideas about flags.

flags

- They have colors.
- They have patterns.
- They wave in the air.
- Every country has one.

Directions: Draw and write about your country's flag. Include at least one fact. Use your notes from page 41 to help you. Then, fill in the checklist.

☑ Checklist

- ☐ Sentences begin with capital letters.
- ☐ Sentences end with punctuation.
- ☐ There are spaces between the words.

Directions: Solve each problem.

1. 4 + 4 = ______

2. $\begin{array}{r} 5 \\ +\ 1 \\ \hline \end{array}$ ☐

3. 5 + 2 = ______

4. $\begin{array}{r} 6 \\ +\ 0 \\ \hline \end{array}$ ☐

5. 7 + 1 = ______

6. $\begin{array}{r} 3 \\ +\ 4 \\ \hline \end{array}$ ☐

7. 8 + 1 = ______

8. $\begin{array}{r} 3 \\ +\ 5 \\ \hline \end{array}$ ☐

9. 3 + 3 ______

10. $\begin{array}{r} 4 \\ +\ 5 \\ \hline \end{array}$ ☐

11. 2 + 5 ______

12. $\begin{array}{r} 9 \\ +\ 0 \\ \hline \end{array}$ ☐

Directions: Use the tally chart to answer each question.

Favorite Type of Movie

Funny	Cartoon	Scary	3-D
|||	~~||||~~ |||	|	~~||||~~

1. How many chose 3-D?

2. How many chose cartoon?

3. How many liked 3-D and scary?

4. Which type of movie is liked least?

5. Which type of movie is liked most?

6. How many more chose funny than scary?

Directions: Look at the example. Then, solve the problem.

Example: Bus A has 25 students. Bus B has 19 students. Which bus has more students?

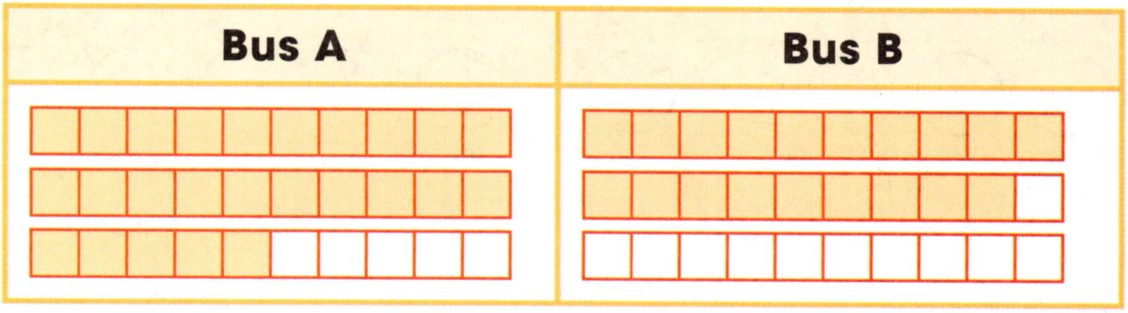

25 > 19

Bus __A__ has more students.

1. Cart A has 21 food items. Cart B has 31 food items. Which cart has more food items?

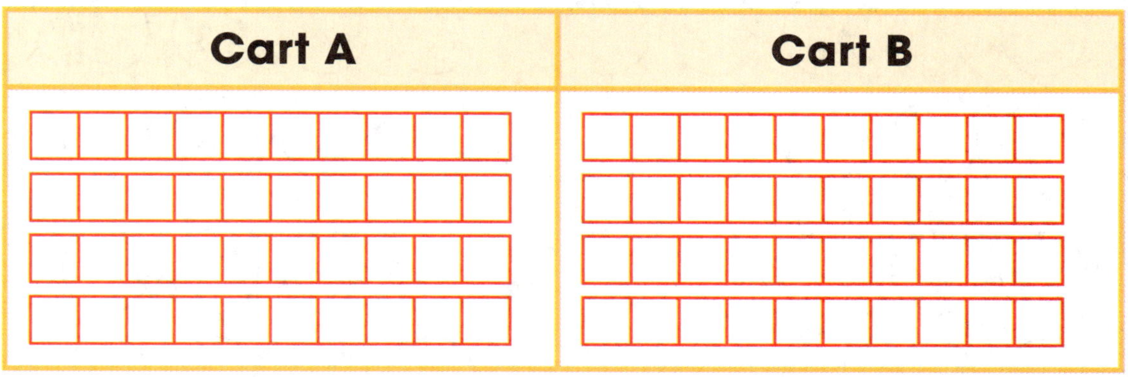

21 ◯ **31**

Cart ________ has more food items.

Directions: Solve the problem by coloring the ten frames.

Show 47 and 44. Use >, <, or = to compare the numbers.

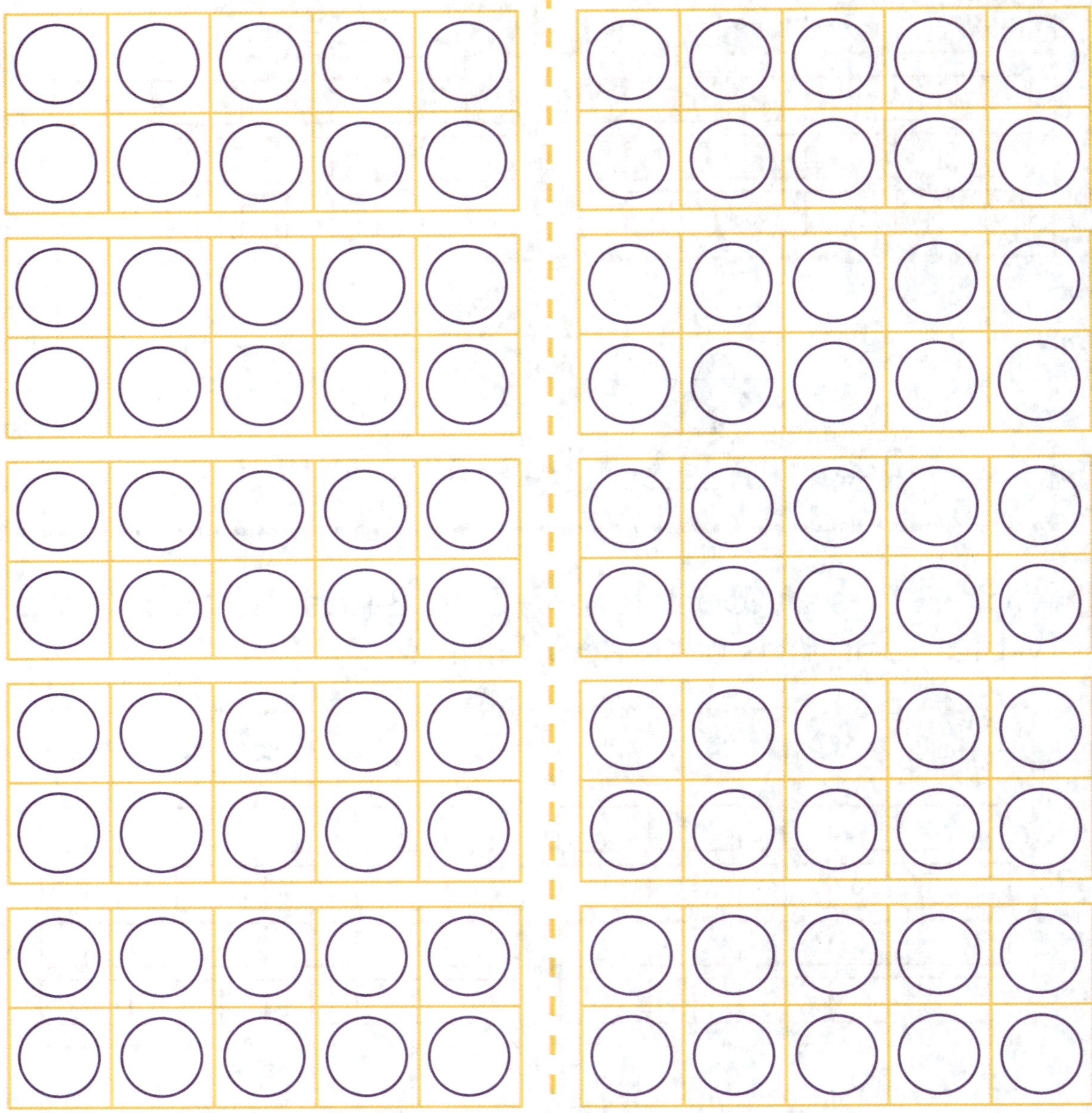

47 ◯ 44

Directions: Circle the letter in the correct column to show if each person or place provides a good or service. Then, answer each question.

	Good	Service
1 barber	*	S
2 grocery store	E	G
3 car wash	O	R
4 furniture store	V	O
5 dry cleaner	D	I
6 dentist	S	C
7 gas station	E	*

8 Write the letters you circled to find the secret word. Be sure to write them in order.

____ ____ ____ ____ ____ ____ ____

9 Write the symbols or letters you did not circle to find another secret word! Be sure to write them in order.

____ ____ ____ ____ ____ ____ ____

Directions: Follow the steps to see how you can cut a string without scissors. Have an adult help you.

What You Need

- length of string
- clear jar with lid
- tape
- magnifying glass

What to Do

1. Tape one end of the string to the inside of the lid.
2. Put the lid back on the jar with the string inside the jar.
3. Place the jar on a flat surface in bright sunlight. Hold a magnifying glass close to the jar so the sun's rays are focused on the string. Be careful not to touch the jar.
4. What happens?

Think About It!

What would it be like if you had to use the sun's energy to cut everything you needed instead of using scissors?

Directions: Change one letter in each answer to answer the next clue. Start by changing the word *him*.

Start: **him**

1. This is a kind of meat.
2. You wear this on your head.
3. This is an animal.
4. You wipe your feet on it.
5. It shows the way.
6. This is something you clean with.
7. This means the opposite of *bottom*.
8. Add a letter to write the opposite of *go*.

Directions: Roll two number cubes. Add the two numbers. Make a tally mark next to the word you rolled. Read the word aloud. Keep rolling until you have read each word at least twice.

Words	Tally Marks
7 = two	
8 = some	
9 = about	
10 = said	
11 = use	
12 = there	

High-Frequency Words Activity

Sort the high-frequency words from page 39 in some way. For example, you can sort them by the number of letters or the number of vowels. How many ways can you sort them? Explain to a family member how you sorted the words.

Writing Activity

Ask a family member about your country's flag. Add one detail you learned to your writing on page 42.

Problem-Solving Activity

Work with a partner. Ask him or her to name a number between 1 and 100. Then, name another number. Write an expression using the two numbers and a <, >, or = sign. Repeat the activity with other numbers.

Critical-Thinking Activity

Write the word *cake* at the top of a sheet of paper. Change only one letter at a time to make new words. Challenge yourself to make 10 new words.

Listening-and-Speaking Activity

Talk to your family members about what they do for work. Talk about whether they provide goods or services.

Directions: Read the text, and answer the questions.

Missing Turtle

Kim says, "Mom, can you help me find my turtle? He is missing."

Mom says, "I think Tork is hiding."

"Why?" asks Kim.

"Winter is coming. Box turtles sleep most of the winter," says Mom.

Kim and Mom find Tork in the closet. Kim asks, "When will he wake up?"

Mom says, "Tork will wake up when he is hungry."

1. What is the name of the turtle?
   - (A) Kim
   - (B) Tork
   - (C) Box

2. When do box turtles sleep?
   - (A) when they are hungry
   - (B) when someone is looking for them
   - (C) in the winter

3. Why is Tork in the closet?
   - (A) to eat
   - (B) to get dressed
   - (C) to sleep

4. What has Kim learned?
   - (A) Turtles can sleep for months.
   - (B) Turtles like winter.
   - (C) Turtles like to be pets.

Directions: Read the text, and answer the questions.

No More Germs

It is hard to keep from getting a cold. You cannot see cold germs. Germs can live for days on things you may touch. Most colds are passed by germs on hands. You can use special wipes that kill germs. But the best way to get rid of germs is by washing your hands.

1. What does getting a *cold* mean?
   - (A) becoming sick
   - (B) feeling chilly
   - (C) getting a coat
2. Why is it hard not to get a cold?
   - (A) Germs die quickly.
   - (B) Germs are easy to see.
   - (C) Germs cannot be seen.
3. How might you get a cold germ?
   - (A) by touching something with germs
   - (B) by eating some foods
   - (C) by touching something clean
4. How do you get most colds?
   - (A) from germs on your hands
   - (B) by getting wet and cold
   - (C) from too much water

Directions: Color each box using the code.

Code	
green—would	**yellow**—write
red—their	**purple**—been
blue—girl	**brown**—first

first	girl	been	their
been	their	write	first
their	would	first	would
write	been	been	girl
girl	their	would	write

Directions: Answer each question.

1. Circle the verb.

   I went under the desk.

2. Write the verb.

   The frog ______________.
   (green or hops)

3. Write the past tense verb.

   The bird ______________ its wings.
   (move or moved)

4. Write the correct verb.

   The rain ______________ no recess.
   (mean or means)

5. Circle the verb.

   I found a coin on the floor.

Directions: Write the name of a holiday you like in each circle. Color the circle with your favorite holiday. Then, write two reasons why you like that holiday.

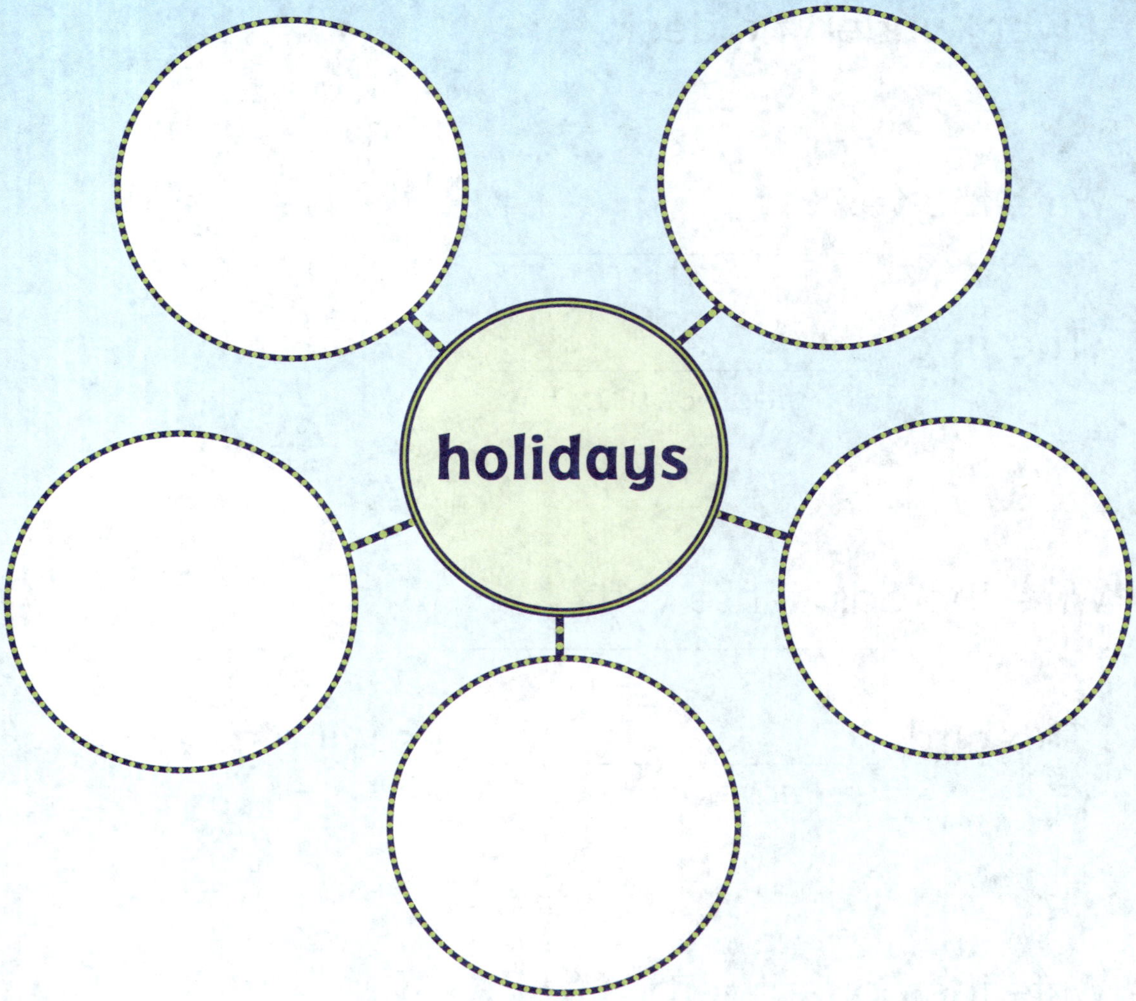

Reason 1

____

Reason 2

____

Directions: Draw and write about your favorite holiday. Include reasons why you like it. Use your notes from page 56 to help you. Then, fill in the checklist.

Opinion

I like ______________________________.

Reasons

____

____

Checklist

- ☐ Sentences begin with capital letters.
- ☐ Sentences end with punctuation.
- ☐ There are spaces between the words.

Directions: Solve each problem.

1.
$$\begin{array}{r} 7 \\ -\ 2 \\ \hline \square \end{array}$$

2. 6 – 5 = ______

3.
$$\begin{array}{r} 8 \\ -\ 8 \\ \hline \square \end{array}$$

4. 9 – 7 = ______

5.
$$\begin{array}{r} 6 \\ -\ 2 \\ \hline \square \end{array}$$

6. 9 – 3 = ______

7.
$$\begin{array}{r} 8 \\ -\ 4 \\ \hline \square \end{array}$$

8. 7 – 1 = ______

9.
$$\begin{array}{r} 4 \\ -\ 3 \\ \hline \square \end{array}$$

10. 6 – 4 = ______

11.
$$\begin{array}{r} 2 \\ -\ 1 \\ \hline \square \end{array}$$

12. 8 – 5 = ______

Directions: Solve each problem.

1. Write the missing number.

   69 70 ______ 72

2. Circle the larger number. 58 52

3. Circle the smaller number. 49 50

4. Write the number before and after 37.

Before	Number	After
	37	

5. Put these numbers in order from least to greatest.

   88, 91, 80

   ______ ______ ______

6. Put these numbers in order from greatest to least.

   29, 32, 21

   ______ ______ ______

Directions: Look at the example. Then, solve the problem by adding.

Example: 15 – 9 = ☐

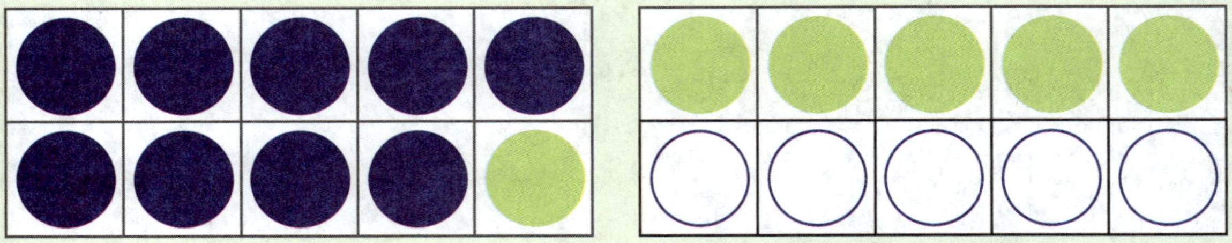

9 + ___6___ = 15

15 – 9 = ___6___

17 – 8 = ☐

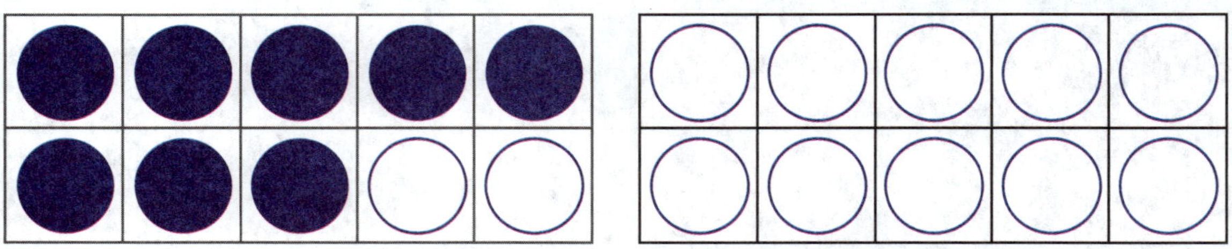

8 + ________ = 17

17 – 8 = ________

Directions: Solve the problem using the ten frames.

Sal has 20 books. He donates 9 of the books to a library. How many books does Sal have now?

○	○	○	○	○
○	○	○	○	○

○	○	○	○	○
○	○	○	○	○

_____ + _____ = _____

_____ − _____ = _____

_____ books

Challenge!

Sal buys 5 new books. How many books does Sal have now?

_____ books

Directions: Time lines are used to show the order of events. Create a time line of your life. Draw or write about something important that happened to you each year.

Birth–Age 1	
Ages 2–3	
Ages 4–5	
Ages 6–7	

Directions: Follow the steps in this experiment to discover how the moon changes.

What You Need

pencil

What to Do

1. Check the moon once a week for four weeks. Draw it each week.

Week 1	Week 2
Week 3	**Week 4**

2. What do you notice?

Directions: Every mini grid must have each shape. Every row must have each shape. Every column must have each shape. 

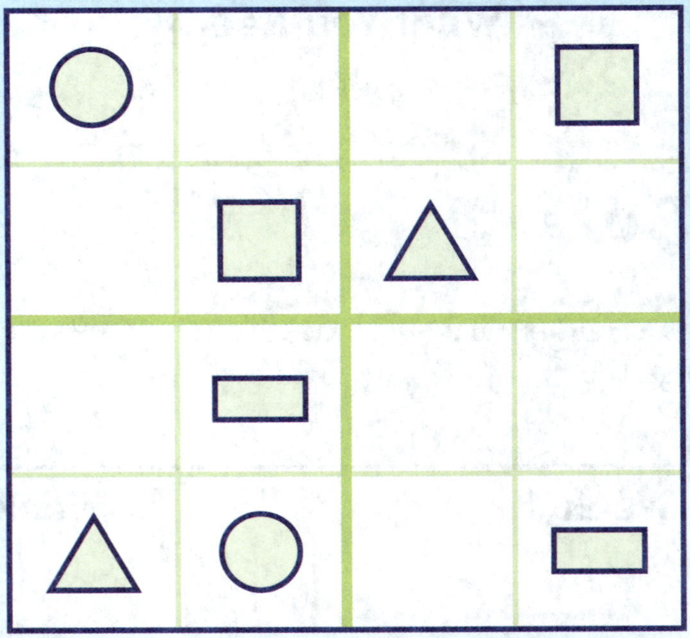

Directions: Every mini grid must have a *1, 2, 3,* and *4.* Every row must have a *1, 2, 3,* and *4.* Every column must have a *1, 2, 3,* and *4.*

	1		2
2	4	3	
1			
		1	3

Directions: Play a pantomime game. Add other holidays people celebrate to the chart. Write the names of these holidays on slips of paper. Put the slips in a container. Choose a slip. Act out the holiday without talking. Have a partner try to guess the holiday.

Valentine's Day 	St. Patrick's Day 	Ramadan 
Hanukkah 	Martin Luther King Jr. Day 	New Year's Eve 
Halloween 	Thanksgiving 	Christmas 

Language Activity

Reread your writing on page 57. Circle the verbs you used. Change any verbs you can to be more active.

Mathematics Activity

Use your lunch or dinner to make a subtraction problem. For example, "I have 10 baby carrots. I eat 4 of them. How many do I still have to eat?"

Problem-Solving Activity

Draw pictures to show two addition and two subtraction facts using the numbers 13, 4, and 9.

Social Studies Activity

Make a time line of your day. Include important events from the day. Explain your time line to a family member.

Critical-Thinking Activity

Make a blank sudoku template. Use four of the sight words from page 54 to create your own puzzle.

Listening-and-Speaking Activity

Explain your observations from page 63 to a family member. Ask your family member if he or she has observed the same thing.

Directions: Read the text, and answer the questions.

The Best Hike

Drew and Bree go on a hike in the mountains. They pack their lunches and gear into backpacks. Drew and Bree snack on trail mix on their hike. A chipmunk darts out and steals a peanut.

After a few hours, they stop and eat their lunch. All of a sudden, Drew whispers, "Look!" There in the clearing, they spot a deer and her fawn. Drew and Bree hold still until the deer leave.

Bree says, "That was the best!"

1. Where are Drew and Bree going?
   - (A) the mountains to ski
   - (B) the mountains to ice skate
   - (C) the mountains to hike

2. Why do they put their gear in backpacks?
   - (A) so they have their gear with them
   - (B) so they can leave their gear
   - (C) so they can fit the gear into the van

3. Why do you think Drew whispers?
   - (A) so the deer won't be scared
   - (B) so Bree won't be scared
   - (C) so Bree won't eat

4. Which sentence best tells about this text?
   - (A) Bree and Drew have their lunch.
   - (B) Bree and Drew go for a hike and see deer.
   - (C) Bree and Drew have the best day.

Directions: Read the text, and answer the questions.

A New Toy

One winter day, Sherman Poppen saw his daughter stand on her sled. Mr. Poppen had an idea. He tied two skis together. His daughter stood on it and rode it down the hill. Then, he added a rope to the front. Now, it could be controlled. It was even more fun to ride. All the children wanted one. Mr. Poppen's wife called the new toy a *snurfer*. A toy company made them. Later, people thought of ways to make them better. You may have used what came next: the snowboard!

1. What did Mr. Poppen use for his idea?
   - (A) a sled
   - (B) his workshop
   - (C) two skis

2. What did Mr. Poppen make?
   - (A) something to sit on
   - (B) something to stand on
   - (C) something to lie on

3. How did Mr. Poppen make the skis better?
   - (A) He added a rope to the front.
   - (B) He added a rope to the back.
   - (C) He added a handle.

4. Why did people make changes to the snurfer?
   - (A) so it would work better
   - (B) so it would be smaller
   - (C) so it could be painted

Directions: Draw a line from each picture to the word that rhymes with it.

1. could

2. rain

3. come

4. may

5. what

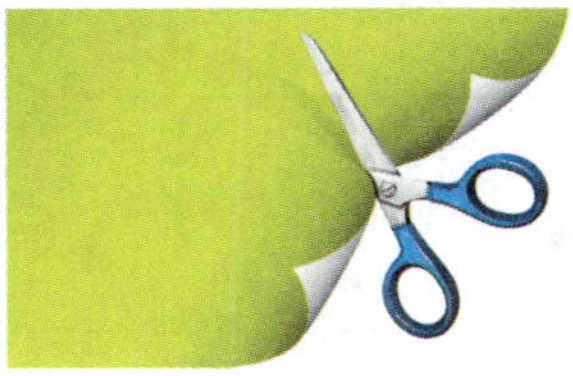

6. new

UNIT 5

Language

Directions: Answer each question.

1. Circle the pronoun.

   I want a new bike.

2. Write the correct pronoun.

   Dad told ____________ to go to sleep.
   (me or I)

3. Write the correct pronoun.

   Pam left, but ____________ forgot her lunch.
   (he or she)

4. Add a pronoun.

   ____________ played in the backyard all day.

5. Circle the pronoun.

   We love to play outside.

Directions: Think about a vacation you took. Complete the chart with notes about it. Then, draw pictures of two events from the day.

Who?	
Where?	
When?	

Event 1	Event 2

Directions: Draw and write about a vacation you took. Use your notes on page 71. Then, fill in the checklist.

Checklist

- ☐ Sentences begin with capital letters.
- ☐ Sentences end with punctuation.
- ☐ There are spaces between the words.

Directions: Solve each problem.

1. 3 + 9 = ______

2. $\begin{array}{r} 7 \\ +\ 3 \\ \hline \end{array}$ ☐

3. 7 + 5 = ______

4. $\begin{array}{r} 10 \\ +\ 5 \\ \hline \end{array}$ ☐

5. 7 + 6 = ______

6. $\begin{array}{r} 9 \\ +\ 5 \\ \hline \end{array}$ ☐

7. 8 + 2 = ______

8. $\begin{array}{r} 8 \\ +\ 5 \\ \hline \end{array}$ ☐

9. 11 + 3 = ______

10. $\begin{array}{r} 13 \\ +\ 4 \\ \hline \end{array}$ ☐

11. 8 + 7 = ______

12. $\begin{array}{r} 12 \\ +\ 6 \\ \hline \end{array}$ ☐

Directions: Solve each problem.

1. Is the mass equal? Circle: yes no

2. Circle the longest line.

3. Record the line length.

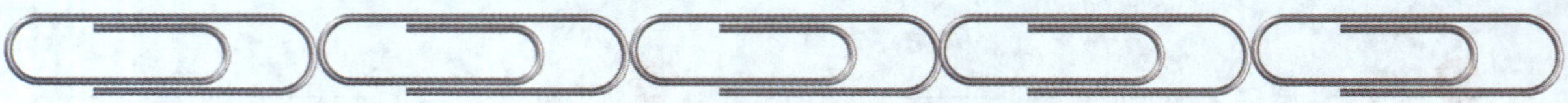

______ paper clips

4. Record the line length.

______ clothespins

5. Record the line length.

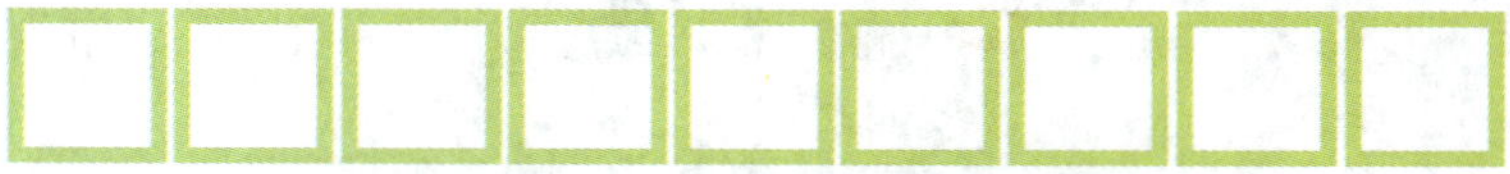

______ squares

Directions: Read the problem. Color the hundreds chart blue to show 45. Color 12 more red to solve the problem.

Kate has 45 shells. She finds 12 more shells at the beach. How many shells does Kate have now?

1	2	3	4	5	6	7	8	9	10
11	12	13	14	15	16	17	18	19	20
21	22	23	24	25	26	27	28	29	30
31	32	33	34	35	36	37	38	39	40
41	42	43	44	45	46	47	48	49	50
51	52	53	54	55	56	57	58	59	60
61	62	63	64	65	66	67	68	69	70
71	72	73	74	75	76	77	78	79	80
81	82	83	84	85	86	87	88	89	90
91	92	93	94	95	96	97	98	99	100

Kate has ____________ shells now.

Directions: Read and solve the problem.

Problem: There are 65 girls on the swim team. Then, 10 more girls join the team. How many girls are on the team now?

What Do You Know?

______ girls are on the swim team.

______ girls join the swim team.

What Is Your Plan?

How can you use the hundreds chart to count the girls?

1	2	3	4	5	6	7	8	9	10
11	12	13	14	15	16	17	18	19	20
21	22	23	24	25	26	27	28	29	30
31	32	33	34	35	36	37	38	39	40
41	42	43	44	45	46	47	48	49	50
51	52	53	54	55	56	57	58	59	60
61	62	63	64	65	66	67	68	69	70
71	72	73	74	75	76	77	78	79	80
81	82	83	84	85	86	87	88	89	90
91	92	93	94	95	96	97	98	99	100

Solve the Problem!

______ girls are on the team now.

Directions: We follow rules to help keep us safe. Write three rules for your bedroom that will help keep people safe when they come in.

Rules in My Room

1.

2.

3.

Directions: Follow the steps in the experiment to discover how babies are like their parents.

What You Need

- picture of an animal
- picture of the animal as a baby

What to Do

1. Look at both photos.
2. Write three ways the animals are alike and three ways they are different.

Alike

Different

Directions: Think of a way to move your body that begins with each letter of the alphabet.

A ____________

B ____________

C ____________

D ____________

E ____________

F ____________

G ____________

H ____________

I ____________

J ____________

K ____________

L ____________

M ____________

N ____________

O ____________

P ____________

Q ____________

R ____________

S ____________

T ____________

U ____________

V ____________

W ____________

X ____________

Y ____________

Z ____________

UNIT 5

Game

Directions: Make up a game for using a snurfer. Write 3 rules of how **not** to use a snurfer. Then, write three things you **can** do with a snurfer.

How Not to Use a Snurfer

1

2

3

What You Can Do with a Snurfer

1

2

3

Challenge!

Draw a picture of a snurfer.

High-Frequency Words Activity

Write six sentences using the high-frequency words on page 69. Include a different high-frequency word in each sentence.

Writing Activity

Reread your writing on page 72. Circle any pronouns you used. If you did not use any pronouns, find a place in your writing where you can add one.

Mathematics Activity

Collect five stuffed animals. Line up them up from shortest to tallest. Then, organize them in some other way.

Problem-Solving Activity

Use the hundreds chart on page 75. Close your eyes, and point to a number with your finger. Open your eyes, and add 12 to that number. Write an equation to show the numbers you added.

Critical-Thinking Activity

Think of an animal or baby animal name for each letter of the alphabet. Create a list like the one on page 79.

Listening-and-Speaking Activity

Tell a friend or family member what your dream vacation would be. Include why you would like this vacation and what you would do for fun.

Directions: Read the text, and answer the questions on the next page.

Dog Heroes

Has there been an earthquake? Did a bad storm hit? Did a hiker get lost on a mountain? That is when some dogs go to work. They are called search and rescue dogs. Dogs have a much better sense of smell than people have. They have been trained to use those noses. Dogs have found people buried under snow or buildings. They are real heroes!

Directions: Read "Dog Heroes," and then answer the questions.

1. When does a search and rescue dog go to work?
   - (A) when their owners have the time
   - (B) when people are lost or missing
   - (C) when they are heroes

2. Why are dogs good at searches?
   - (A) They are strong and work hard.
   - (B) They can smell things that are buried.
   - (C) They like to hunt and run.

3. How can you tell the dog in the photograph is working?
   - (A) He is outside.
   - (B) He is wearing a rescue vest.
   - (C) He looks cute.

4. What is another good title for this text?
   - (A) "Dogs on the Run!"
   - (B) "Dogs and People"
   - (C) "Dogs to the Rescue!"

Directions: Complete each sentence with a word from the Word Bank.

Word Bank

- take
- only
- sound
- over
- little
- know

1. Look at the ________________ dog!
2. Go ________________ the hill.
3. I ________________ how to hop.
4. What is that ________________?
5. ________________ take one bun.
6. Can I ________________ one?

Directions: Answer each question.

1. Circle the word that is spelled correctly.

   com cume come

2. Circle the words that are spelled correctly.

   every rownd walk

3. Write the correct word.

   Please put the cup ______________________.
   (*her or here*)

4. Write two words with the *–ill* pattern, as in *bill*.

   ______________________ ______________________

5. Circle the word that is spelled correctly.

   your yor ur

6. Write the correct word.

   My friend is over ______________________.
   (*there or where*)

Directions: Think about birds. Read the ideas in the web. Then, add three more ideas of your own.

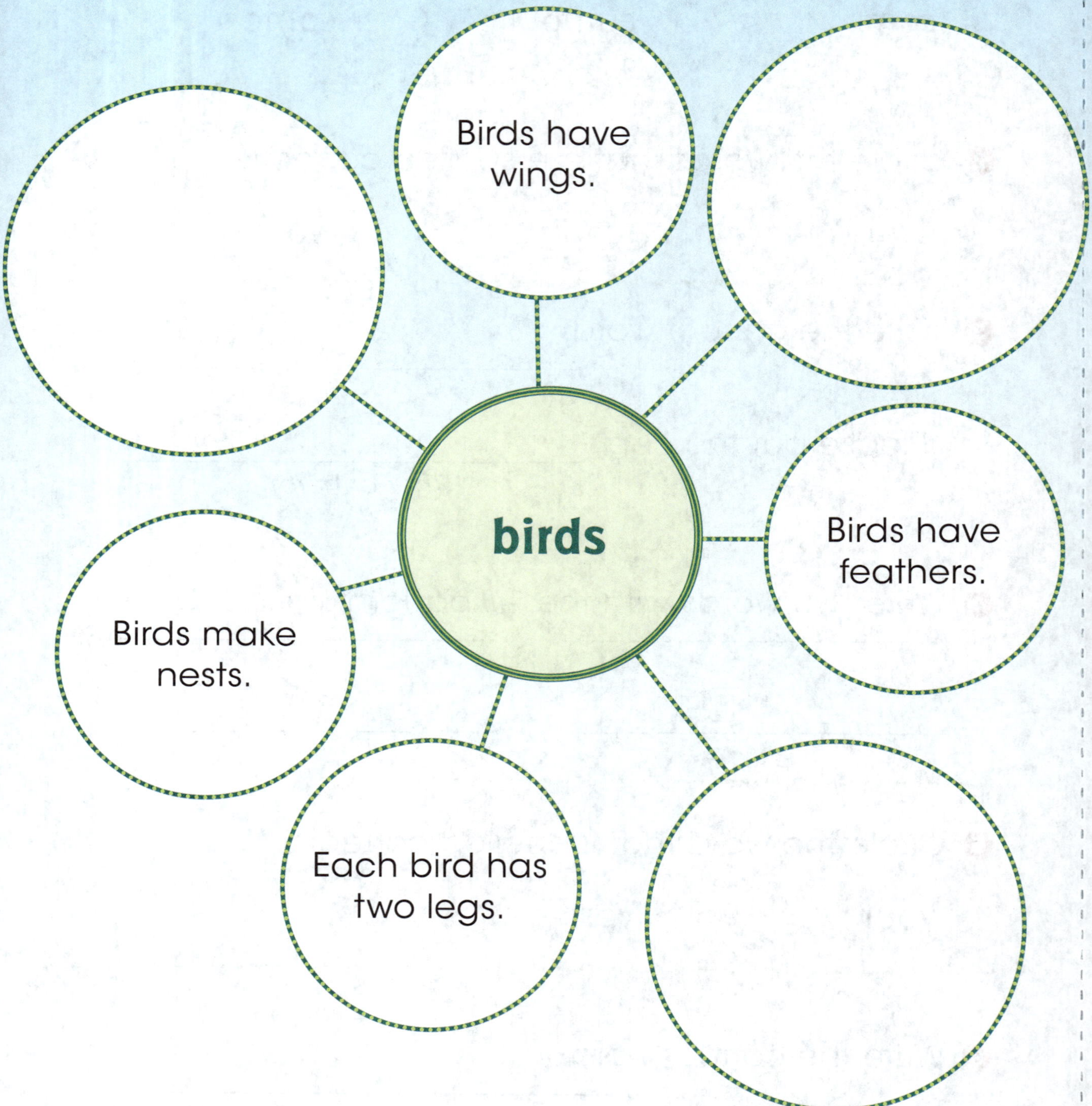

Directions: Draw and write about a bird. Include at least one fact. Use your notes from page 86 to help you. Then, fill in the checklist.

Checklist

- [ ] Sentences begin with capital letters.
- [ ] Sentences end with punctuation.
- [ ] There are spaces between the words.

Directions: Solve each problem.

1. $\begin{array}{r} 15 \\ -\ 10 \\ \hline \end{array}$ ☐

2. 11 – 8 = ______

3. $\begin{array}{r} 14 \\ -\ 4 \\ \hline \end{array}$ ☐

4. 15 – 7 = ______

5. $\begin{array}{r} 12 \\ -\ 11 \\ \hline \end{array}$ ☐

6. 16 – 0 = ______

7. $\begin{array}{r} 19 \\ -\ 4 \\ \hline \end{array}$ ☐

8. 15 – 4 = ______

9. $\begin{array}{r} 18 \\ -\ 6 \\ \hline \end{array}$ ☐

10. 14 – 7 = ______

11. $\begin{array}{r} 17 \\ -\ 12 \\ \hline \end{array}$ ☐

12. 15 – 14 = ______

UNIT 6

Mathematics

Directions: Solve each problem.

1. $7 + 2 + 5 = \square$

2. 4 + 4 + 4 = ______

3. $6 + 2 + 2 = \square$

4. 4 + 5 + 4 = ______

5. $6 + 7 + 5 = \square$

6. 7 + 3 + 7 = ______

7. $8 + 2 + 4 = \square$

8. 7 + 1 + 3 = ______

9. $9 + 2 + 5 = \square$

10. 4 + 1 + 6 = ______

11. $6 + 3 + 4 = \square$

12. 4 + 5 + 5 = ______

Directions: Read and solve the problem.

Sofia asks her friends, "What is your favorite color?" She wrote their answers on a notepad.

green	red	blue	blue	green
red	blue	green	blue	red
blue	blue	blue	red	green

1. Make a tally chart of Sofia's votes.

Color	Tally of Votes

2. How many fewer friends picked green than blue?

_______ friends

3. How many friends did Sofia ask?

_______ friends

Directions: Draw lines to solve the problem.

1. How can this shape be made using only trapezoids?

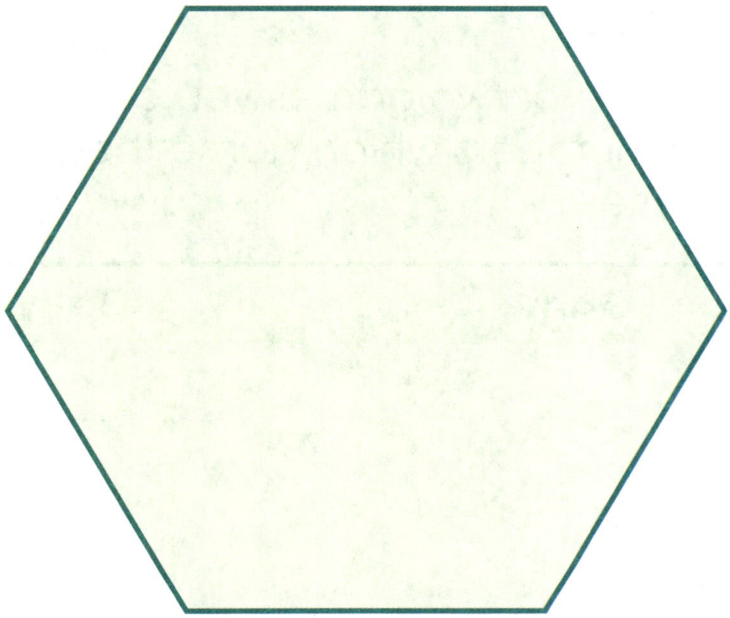

2. How can this shape be made using only triangles?

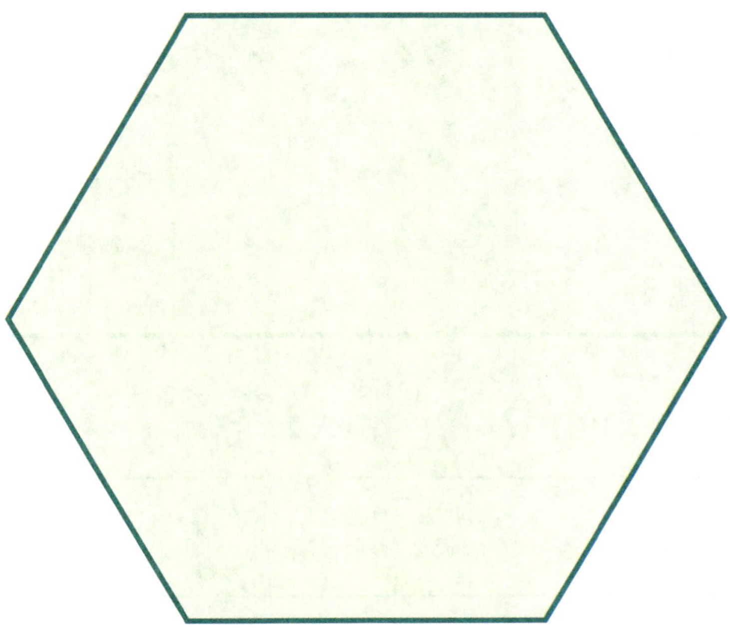

Directions: We vote to make decisions. The most votes wins! Follow the steps to take a vote.

1. Plan a game night with your family. Take a vote to see what game you will play.

2. Write the name of two games you could play. Ask your family members which game they want to play. Tally their votes.

Game	Tally of Votes

3. Which game won?

____

4. Play the winning game with your family.

Directions: Follow the steps in the experiment to discover how sound works.

What You Need

- a balloon
- speakers

What to Do

1. Place your fingers against your throat. Start talking. What do you feel?

2. Blow up the balloon, and tie the end. Play music through the speakers. Hold the balloon in front of you. Move toward the music. What can you feel?

3. Use both hands to hold the balloon against your ear. Have someone else talk to you. What do you hear?

4. What happened whenever there was a sound?

Directions: Name the opposite of each word.

1. old
2. weak
3. narrow
4. rough
5. dark
6. difficult
7. expensive
8. shallow
9. poor
10. tight

Directions: Write the opposite of each high-frequency word below. Then, watch TV or read a book for a half an hour. Make a tally mark each time you hear or read one of the words you wrote.

Words	Tally Marks
Opposite of *take:*	
Opposite of *over:*	
Opposite of *little:*	

1. Which word has the most tally marks?

2. Which word has the least tally marks?

High-Frequency Words Activity

Write a short story using all the high-frequency words on page 84.

Writing Activity

Have an adult help you find one more fact about birds. Add this fact to your writing on page 87.

Mathematics Activity

Write the numbers 0–9 on small slips of paper. Put the slips into a container. Pull three slips out of the container. Add the three numbers together. Explain the strategy you used to add.

Social Studies Activity

Ask an adult about a time he or she voted. Ask this person how he or she decided what or who to vote for.

Critical-Thinking Activity

List as many pairs of opposites as you can think of in two minutes.

Listening-and-Speaking Activity

Discuss the science experiment from page 93 with a family member. Explain to him or her what you observed.

Directions: Read the text, and answer the questions on the next page.

Frozen Sights

Mara and Joe are on a field trip. Their class is at the Cave of the Winds. They go very deep into the cave on the tour. It is so dark that they need to carry a lantern to see. Joe and Mara walk carefully through the cave. Some of the trail is wet and slippery. They have to squeeze through some narrow places. It is dark and still. The only light comes from the lanterns.

The class sees rocks of all kinds of shapes. They see big things that look like icicles. They are called stalactites. They hang down from the ceiling of the cave. Some rocks come up from the ground. Some walls look like frozen waterfalls. Mara and Joe are glad they wore their coats! They like the tour, but they are glad when they come out of the cave and get back to the sunshine. It is cold down there!

Directions: Read "Frozen Sights," and then answer the questions.

1. Why is it dark on the tour?
   - (A) They are deep under the ground.
   - (B) They are on the tour at night.
   - (C) They are walking without lights.

2. What does a stalactite look like?
   - (A) a huge icicle on the ground
   - (B) a huge icicle on the ceiling
   - (C) a frozen waterfall

3. Why are Mara and Joe glad they have their coats?
   - (A) It is dark in the cave.
   - (B) It is cold in the cave.
   - (C) It is quiet in the cave.

4. What does the title "Frozen Sights" mean?
   - (A) Mara and Joe saw things in the cave that looked frozen.
   - (B) Mara and Joe saw things that used to be frozen.
   - (C) Mara and Joe saw dripping icicles in the cave.

Directions: The words in the Word Bank are hidden in code. Use the phone to break the code. Write the words on the lines.

Word Bank

- work
- back
- live
- very
- after

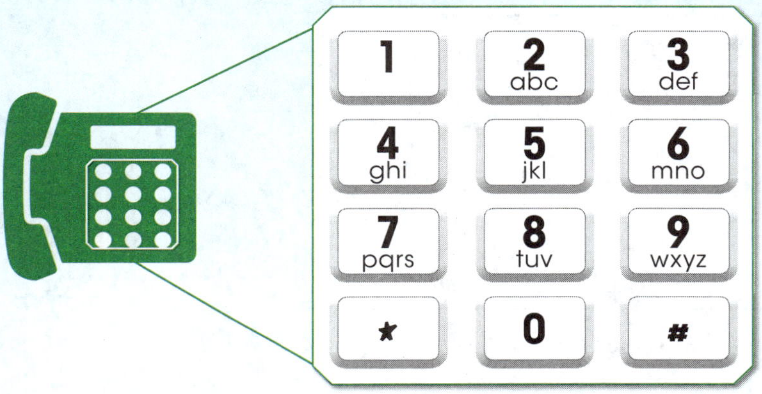

Example:

3 + 6 + 4

d o g

1. 2 + 3 + 8 + 3 + 7 ______________________
2. 8 + 3 + 7 + 9 ______________________
3. 5 + 4 + 8 + 3 ______________________
4. 2 + 2 + 2 + 5 ______________________
5. 9 + 6 + 7 + 5 ______________________

Directions: Write the correct noun in each sentence.

1. The ______________________ feel sad today.
   (girls or girl)

2. The ______________________ stops at the corner.
   (car or cars)

3. The ______________________ look for food.
   (snake or snakes)

4. ______________________ are yellow.
   (Banana or Bananas)

5. The ______________________ wears a red shirt.
   (boy or boys)

6. My ______________________ are small.
   (dog or dogs)

Directions: Write the name of a sport you like to play in each circle. Color the circle with your favorite sport. Then, write two reasons why you like that sport.

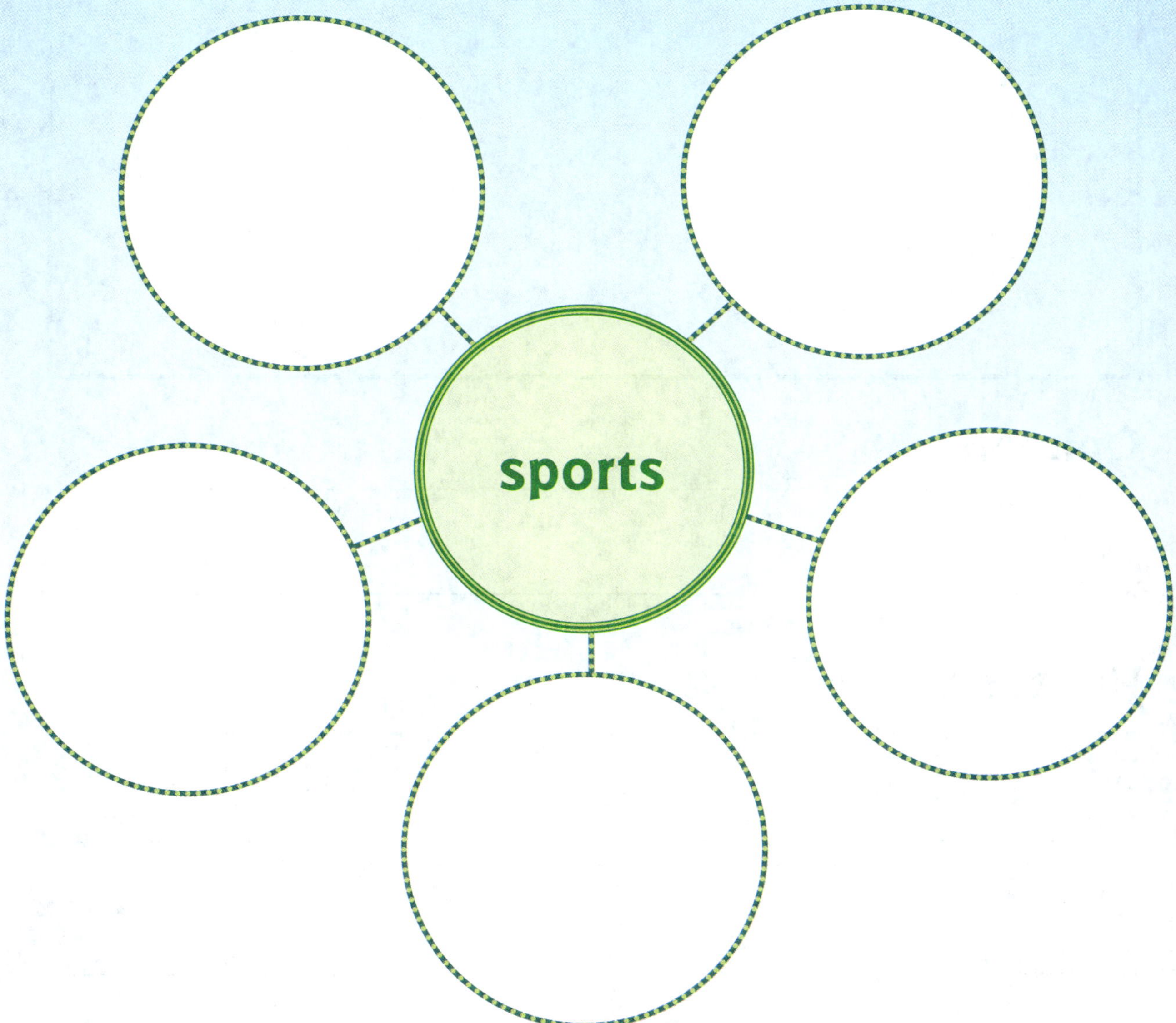

Reason 1

Reason 2

Directions: Draw and write about your favorite sport. Include reasons why you like it. Use your notes from page 101 to help you. Then, fill in the checklist.

Opinion

I like ____________________.

Reasons

____

____

Checklist

- ☐ Sentences begin with capital letters.
- ☐ Sentences end with punctuation.
- ☐ There are spaces between the words.

Directions: Solve each problem.

1. True or false?

   $5 + 6 = 10 + 1$

   ____

2. Circle the ways to make 8.

   6 + 3

   4 + 4

   10 – 2

   12 – 4

3. Write the missing sign.

   $$\begin{array}{r} 8 \\ \square\ 4 \\ \hline 4 \end{array}$$

4. Write the missing sign.

   $6 + 3 = 5 \square 4$

5. Make it true.

   $4 + 1 = 3 + \square$

6. Circle the ways to make 10.

   5 + 5

   2 + 8

   15 – 4

   13 – 3

7. Make it true.

   $5 + 3 = 10 - \square$

8. Write the missing sign.

   $8 \square 2 = 3 + 3$

Directions: Solve each problem.

1. Fill in the circle with <, >, or =.

   78 ◯ 68

2. Fill in the circle with <, >, or =.

   52 ◯ 52

3. Fill in the circle with <, >, or =.

   45 ◯ 64

4. Make the number sentence true.

   38 = ____________

5. Make the number sentence true.

   58 > ____________

6. Make the number sentence true.

   44 < ____________

Directions: Read and solve the problem.

Beckett has 25 baseball cards. Show two ways to group the baseball cards by tens and ones. Draw circles around groups of ten.

Strategy 1

☐ ☐ ☐ ☐ ☐ ☐ ☐ ☐ ☐ ☐

☐ ☐ ☐ ☐ ☐ ☐ ☐ ☐ ☐ ☐

☐ ☐ ☐ ☐ ☐

________ tens and ________ ones

Strategy 2

☐ ☐ ☐ ☐ ☐ ☐ ☐ ☐ ☐ ☐

☐ ☐ ☐ ☐ ☐ ☐ ☐ ☐ ☐ ☐

☐ ☐ ☐ ☐ ☐

________ tens and ________ ones

Directions: Read and solve the problem.

Find 3 objects that are shorter than your foot. Find 3 objects that are about the same length as your foot. Find 3 objects that are longer than your foot.

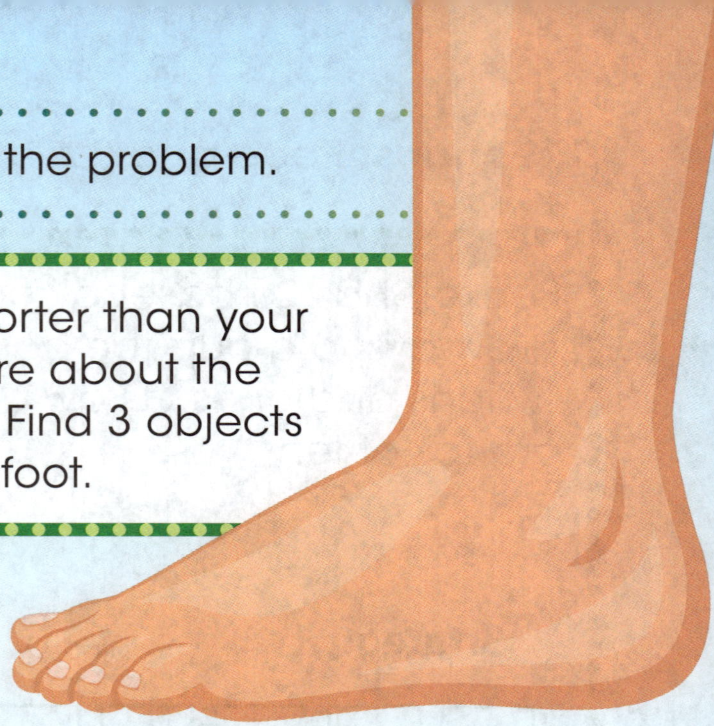

Shorter than my foot	Same length as my foot	Longer than my foot

Directions: Look at the Word Bank. Decide which items are wants and which are needs. Write each word in the correct column. Draw pictures of some of the words.

Word Bank

- water
- TV
- toys
- bike
- clothes
- food
- games
- place to live

Wants	Needs

Directions: Follow the steps with two partners to discover how Earth and the moon move.

What You Need

- two sheets of construction paper
- a marker
- a globe or ball

What to Do

1. Make two signs. Write *sun* on one. Write *moon* on the other.

2. Have a person stand in the center of the room holding the *sun* sign.

3. Have a person hold the globe or ball and walk slowly around the sun in a circle. In space, it takes Earth one year to go around the sun. This means that it takes 365 days.

4. Now, spin the globe or ball. In space, it takes 24 hours for Earth to make one complete spin. What do we call 24 hours?

____

5. Finally, take the moon sign, and walk in a circle around the globe or ball. In space, it takes about a month for the moon to go around Earth.

6. Draw a picture on a sheet of paper that shows how Earth and the moon move. Use arrows to show their motion.

Directions: A *hink pink* is a pair of words that rhymes and solves a riddle. Use the clues to figure out these hink pinks.

Example: What do you call a damp dog?

a wet pet

1. What do you call an unhappy father?

2. What do you call a chubby kitty?

3. What do you call a wealthy woman who casts spells?

4. What do you call a cap that got sat on?

5. What do you call fake hair for a hog?

Directions: Place a paper clip on the X in the left circle. Place a pencil through the paper clip. Spin the paper clip around the pencil. Repeat with the right circle. Record the two-digit number you make on the left line. Spin another two-digit number, and write it on the right line. Fill in the box with >, <, or =.

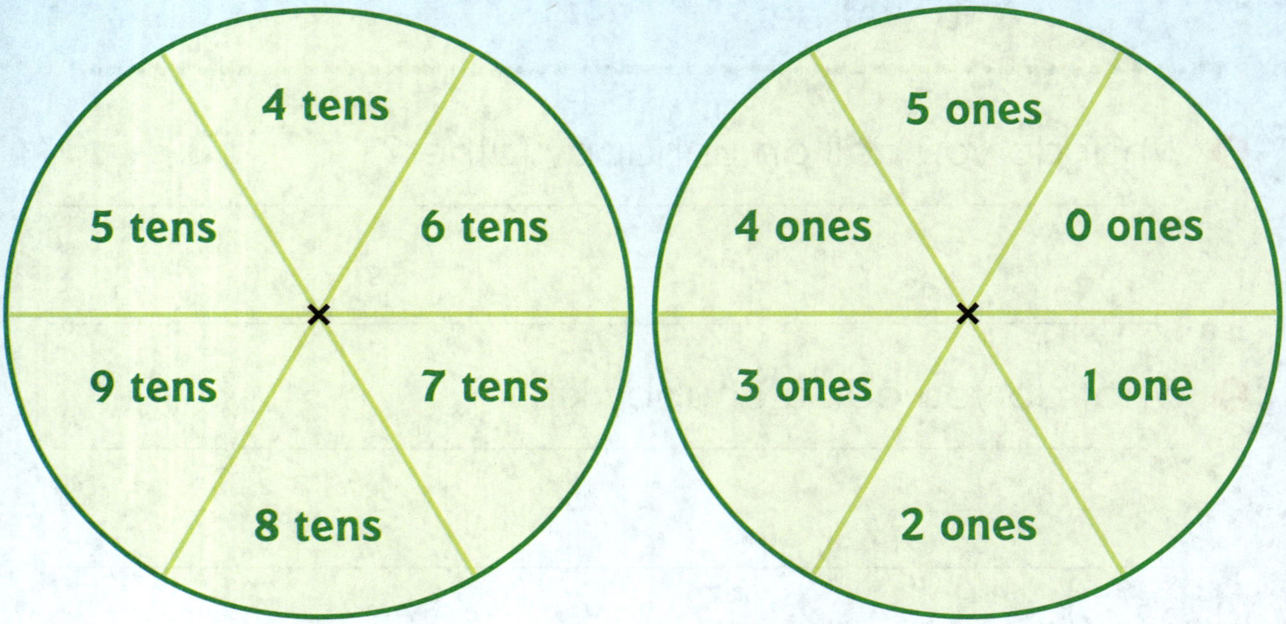

1 ________ ☐ ________

2 ________ ☐ ________

3 ________ ☐ ________

4 ________ ☐ ________

5 ________ ☐ ________

High-Frequency Words Activity

Challenge yourself to write a sentence that uses three out of the six high-frequency words from page 99.

Mathematics Activity

Write expressions that equal 12. For example, you could write 6 + 6 or 14 – 2. Challenge yourself to write at least six expressions.

Problem-Solving Activity

Review the objects that you wrote in the chart on page 106. Write the objects in order from shortest to tallest. Then, write them in a different order.

Social Studies Activity

Make a list of the wants and needs your family has. Compare your list to the chart you completed on page 107.

Critical-Thinking Activity

Create your own hink pinks. Begin by thinking of two rhyming words. Then, think of a question that could be asked to get someone to say the rhyming words.

Listening-and-Speaking Activity

Explain to a friend or family member the way Earth and the moon move. Show him or her your drawing from the lab, and explain how it helped you understand their movements.

Directions: Read the text, and answer the questions on the next page.

Hurricanes: Big Storms

A hurricane is a huge storm. It begins over the ocean. Winds blow in a circle. The winds can blow up to 200 miles (322 kilometers) per hour. It rains hard. But something interesting happens in the middle of a hurricane. The winds do not blow as hard. It does not rain as much. It is pretty calm. This is called the *eye* of the storm.

The winds in a hurricane push the water around. Giant waves form. The sea level can get very high. This is called a storm surge.

Is a hurricane coming? Do you live near the ocean? Then you may need to go somewhere safe until the storm ends. The strong winds can tear up trees. The rain can cause flooding. The sea level may rise with the storm surge. Boats can get tossed around by the waves. The beach may be worn away. If you are caught in a hurricane, do not be fooled by the calm eye of the storm. There is still more hurricane to come!

Directions: Read "Hurricanes: Big Storms," and then answer the questions.

1. Which sentence is true about a hurricane?
   - (A) Strong winds blow in a circle.
   - (B) Light winds blow across the ocean.
   - (C) Strong winds can blow 300 miles per hour.

2. What does the word *hard* mean in this text?
   - (A) mean
   - (B) strongly
   - (C) fast

3. What is the calm part in the center of a hurricane called?
   - (A) the center
   - (B) the eye
   - (C) the calm spot

4. What kind of place would be safe in a hurricane?
   - (A) a big house by the beach
   - (B) a house far away from the beach
   - (C) a park near the ocean

Directions: Read and trace each word. Then, write each word using fancy letters. You can write it *curly*, skinny, or wide.

Normal	Fancy
man	
our	
just	
name	
good	
great	

Directions: Answer each question.

1. Circle the adjective.

   I like to sit in red chairs.

2. Write the adjective.

   The ________________ butterfly flew.
   (pretty or wing)

3. Write an adjective.

   The singer sang a ________________ song.

4. Write two adjectives about a flower.

5. Write two adjectives about a sweater.

Directions: Think about a fun place you went with your family. Complete the chart with notes about the day. Then, draw pictures of two events from the day.

Who?	
Where?	
When?	

Event 1	Event 2

Directions: Draw and write about a fun place you went with your family. Use your ideas from page 116 to help you. Then, fill in the checklist.

Checklist

- ☐ Sentences begin with capital letters.
- ☐ Sentences end with punctuation.
- ☐ There are spaces between the words.

Directions: Solve each problem.

1. $\square + 3 = 7$

2. $\begin{array}{r} 8 \\ - \square \\ \hline 3 \end{array}$

3. $\square + 4 = 8$

4. $\begin{array}{r} 2 \\ + \square \\ \hline 6 \end{array}$

5. $7 + \square = 8$

6. $\begin{array}{r} 2 \\ + \square \\ \hline 4 \end{array}$

7. $10 - \square = 4$

8. $\begin{array}{r} \square \\ - 4 \\ \hline 3 \end{array}$

9. $12 - \square = 2$

10. $\begin{array}{r} \square \\ + 1 \\ \hline 13 \end{array}$

11. $\square + 5 = 5$

12. $\begin{array}{r} 6 \\ - \square \\ \hline 3 \end{array}$

Directions: This picture graph shows which ice cream flavors some kids liked best. Use it to answer each question.

Favorite Ice Cream

Chocolate Ice Cream	
Strawberry Ice Cream	
Vanilla Ice Cream	

1. How many kids chose vanilla?

   ____

2. Which flavor did the fewest kids choose?

   ____

3. Which flavor did most kids choose?

   ____

4. How many more kids chose chocolate than strawberry?

   ____

5. How many kids chose strawberry or vanilla?

   ____

6. How many kids in all chose a flavor?

   ____

Directions: Read and solve the problem.

Mr. Morales has 6 red pens, 7 blue pens, and 4 green pens. He gives away 3 pens. How many pens does Mr. Morales have now?

Draw a picture to show how to solve the problem.

______ pens

Directions: Solve the problem using the ten frames.

Ryan has 90 books. He gives 20 books to his friends. How many books does Ryan have now?

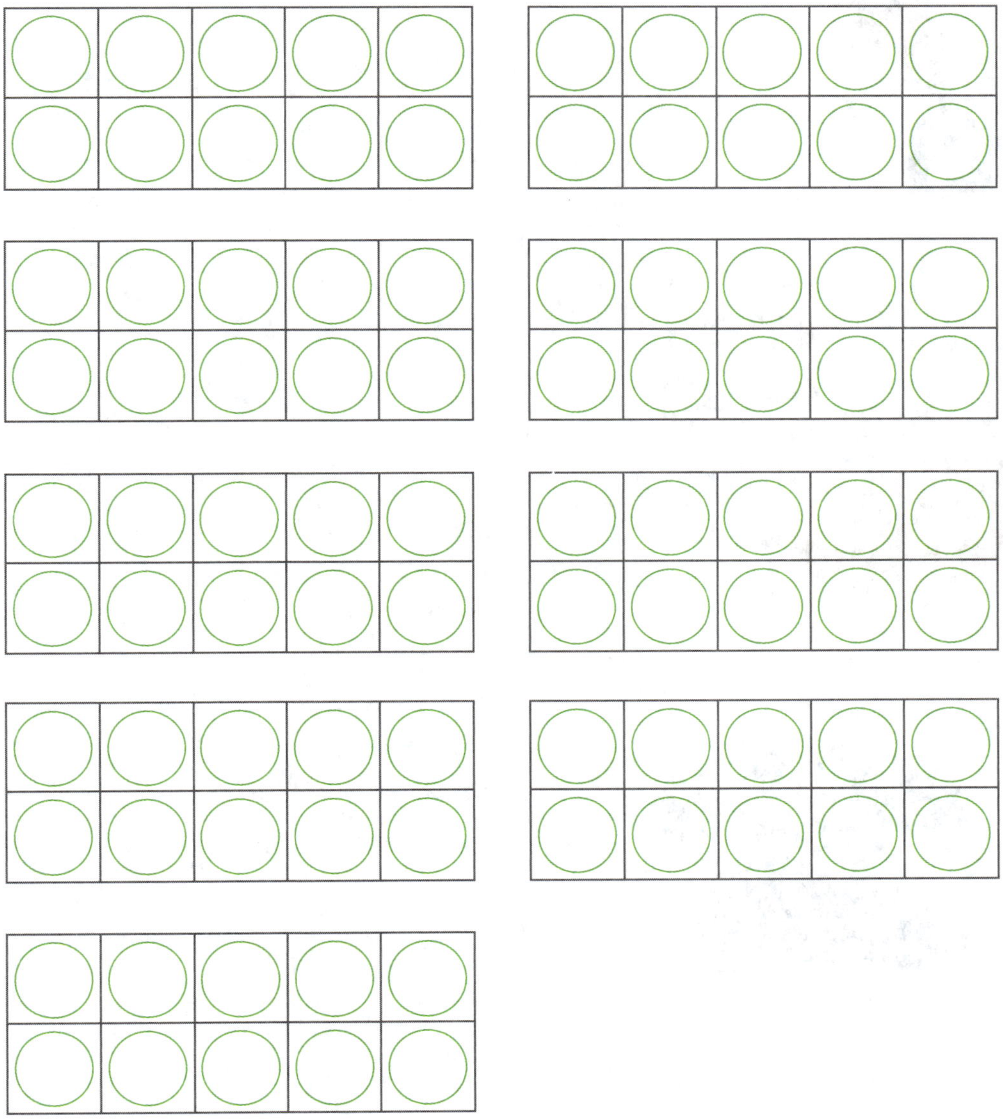

______________ books

Directions: Look at each old-fashioned item. Draw how each item looks today.

1 	
2 	
3 	
4 	

Directions: Follow the steps in the experiment to discover how far plants can reach.

What You Need

- see-through plastic cups
- potting soil
- seeds
- ruler
- water
- craft sticks

What to Do

1. Fill 4 cups two-thirds full with potting soil.
2. Place seeds along each side of the cup. Use a different depth for the seeds in each cup: 2 cm, 4 cm, 6 cm, and 8 cm. Use a craft stick to label each cup with the depth of the seeds.
3. Make sure the seeds are covered with soil. Then, sprinkle water in each cup.
4. Place the cups in a sunny window, and water as needed for two weeks. Draw what you see on a separate sheet of paper.

Think About It!

What would happen if a different number of seeds (2 seeds, 5 seeds, 10 seeds, 20 seeds) were placed in each cup? Which cup of seeds do you think would grow the best? Why?

Directions: Use the clues to figure out each child's favorite fruit. Put a ✓ in the chart to mark each child's favorite fruit.

Clues

- Each child likes a different fruit.
- Pearl likes a fruit that begins with the same letter as her name.
- The fruit Raj likes can be red, green, or yellow.
- The fruit Pete likes has four letters in its name.
- Jamal likes a fruit that is long and skinny.

	Apple	**Pineapple**	**Banana**	**Pear**
Pete				
Jamal				
Raj				
Pearl				

Directions: Play a word game with a partner. For each pair of nouns, say as many adjectives as you can that describe either noun. Challenge yourselves by setting a timer for one minute.

Game 1

hurricane	plant
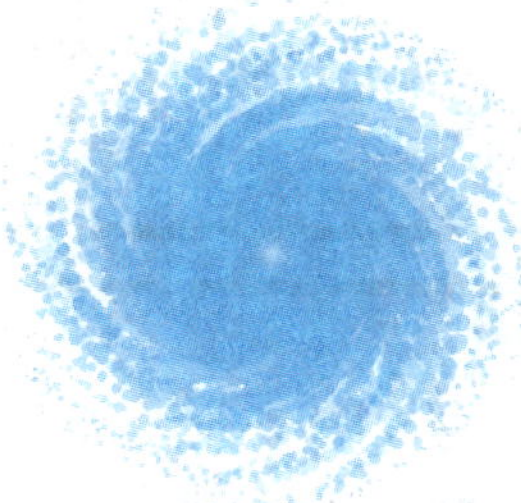	

Game 2

car	house

Game 3

parade	celebration

High-Frequency Words Activity

Use letter tiles or magnets to spell each high-frequency word from page 114. Read each word aloud after you spell it.

Writing Activity

Reread your writing from page 117. Circle any adjectives you included. Add at least two more adjectives to your writing.

Mathematics Activity

Create your own favorite ice cream graph. Ask friends and family what flavors they would choose. Compare your graph to the one on page 119.

Problem-Solving Activity

Practice counting forward and backward by tens. Once you have mastered counting by tens starting at zero, practice starting at another number such as 6 (6, 16, 26, 36, 46, 56, and so on).

Social Studies Activity

Interview an adult about how things have changed since he or she was a child. Ask what things are the same today and what things are different.

Listening-and-Speaking Activity

Teach a family member how to do something. Choose something you enjoy doing, such as how to make a sandwich, or something fun, such as how to play a game.

Directions: Read the text, and answer the questions on the next page.

One Amazing Day

Nick wakes up early on Saturday. "Get up!" he says to Fran. "The amusement park opens in two hours. I want to be first in line at the ticket booth!" Fran pulls back her covers. She is already dressed!

Nick and Fran hurry to the Twister. They want to ride before the roller coaster lines get long. They cling to the car as it climbs to the top and waits. Then, it twists and turns as it races the track. Whee!

The lines are short, so they ride the roller coaster again. Then, they hurry to the Log Ride and get put in the two front seats. Guess what happens? When the log slides to the bottom, they get soaked!

The amusement park has a new ride. Fran and Nick watch it swing high in the air. It swings so high that it looks like it will go in a complete circle. They decide to try it next. They have a long wait, but the ride is worth it. They can see the entire park from the top when they are brave enough to look! What an amazing view! What an amazing day!

Directions: Read "One Amazing Day," and then answer the questions.

1. Where do Nick and Fran go first?
   - (A) the roller coaster
   - (B) the car
   - (C) the track

2. What kind of ride is the log ride?
   - (A) a roller coaster
   - (B) a water ride
   - (C) a train ride

3. What does *soaked* mean in this text?
   - (A) damp
   - (B) cold
   - (C) wet

4. What might Nick and Fran do next?
   - (A) Go on more rides.
   - (B) Go on a treasure hunt.
   - (C) Complain about their bad day.

Directions: Read each word. Circle the hidden word in each row.

1. think

k	h	t	h	i	n	k	t	n	i

2. say

y	s	y	a	s	a	y	a	s	y

3. sentence

t	s	e	n	t	e	n	c	e	n

4. where

e	r	h	r	w	h	e	r	e	w

5. help

p	l	e	h	h	e	l	p	e	l

6. much

m	u	c	h	c	u	m	c	h	u

Directions: Answer each question.

1. Add an *–ing* ending to the base word *say*.

2. Add an *–ed* ending to the base word *help*.

3. Add an *–s* and *–ing* ending to the base word *walk*.

4. Add *–s, -ed,* and *–ing* to the base word *work*.

Directions: Think about kinds of community workers. Read the ideas in the web. Then, add four more ideas of your own.

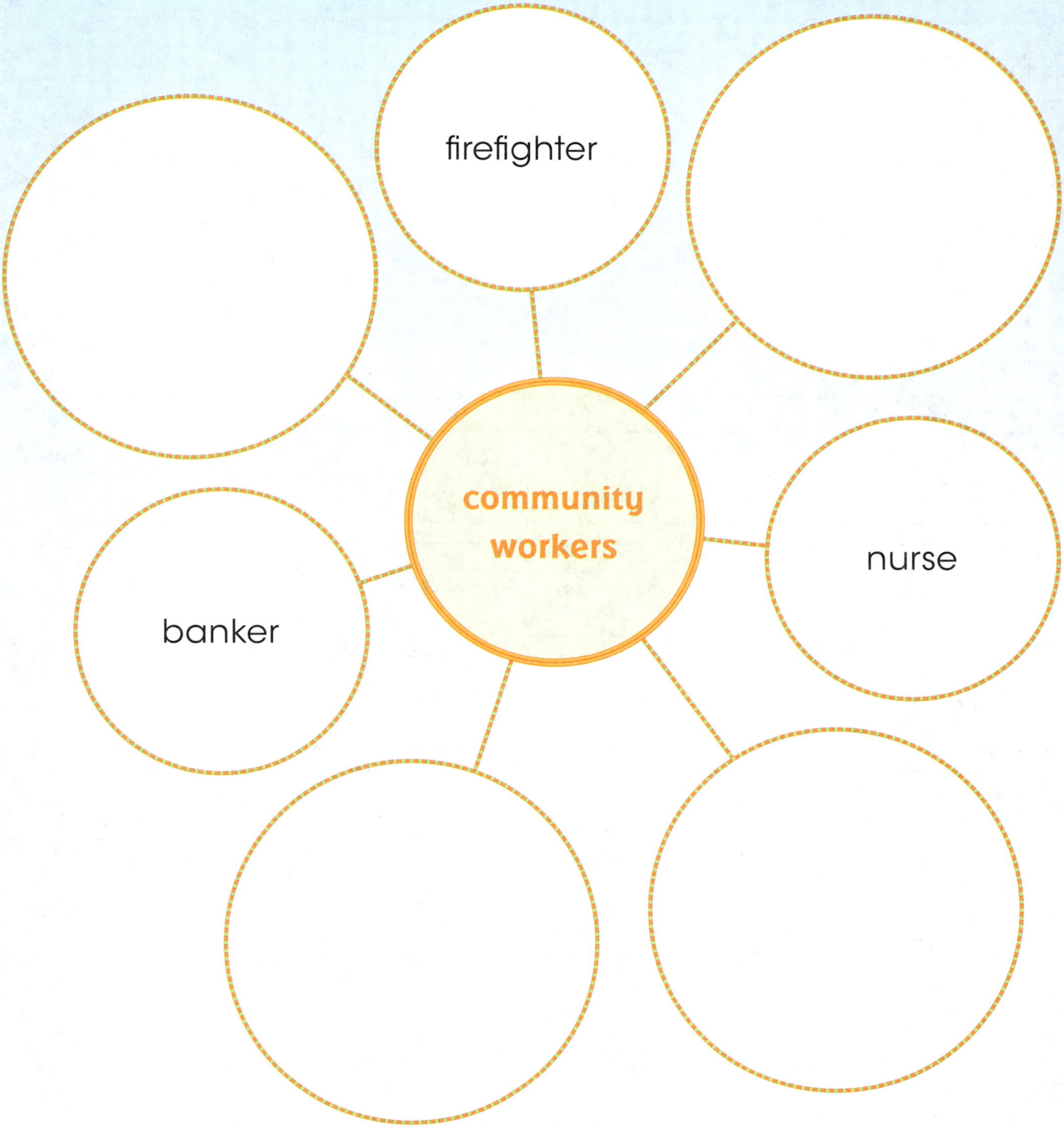

UNIT 9

Writing

Directions: Draw and write about a community worker. Include at least one fact. Use your notes from page 131 to help you. Then, fill in the checklist.

Checklist

- [ ] Sentences begin with capital letters.
- [ ] Sentences end with punctuation.
- [ ] There are spaces between the words.

Directions: Solve each problem.

1. $9 - \square = 2$

7. $12 - \square = 5$

2. $12 - \square = 10$

8. $\square - 8 = 6$

3. $\square - 5 = 6$

9. $18 - \square = 13$

4. $18 - \square = 9$

10. $17 - \square = 10$

5. $15 - \square = 7$

11. $\square - 8 = 3$

6. $9 - \square = 5$

12. $\square - 9 = 7$

Directions: Solve each problem.

1. Draw a line of symmetry.

2. Circle the shape you would see from the top of this prism.

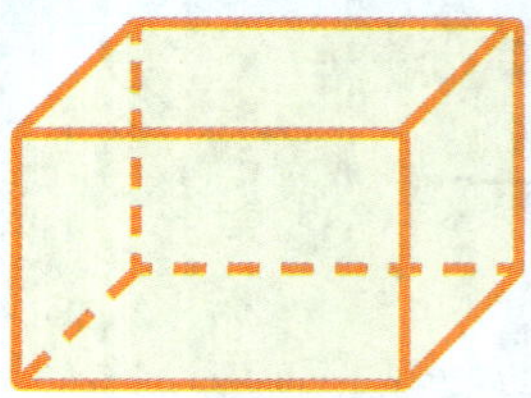

3. Does the solid have any flat surfaces?

Circle: yes no

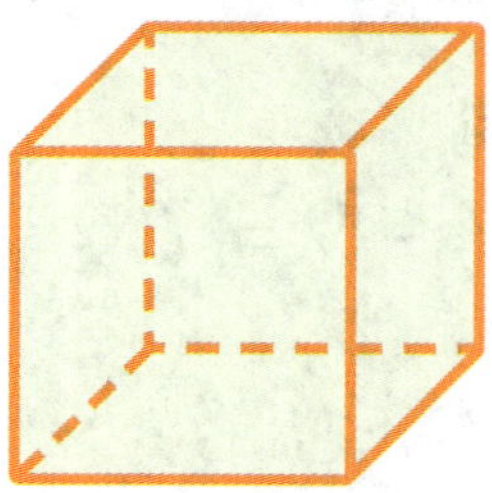

4. Circle the object that is a cube.

5. Circle the object that looks like the solid.

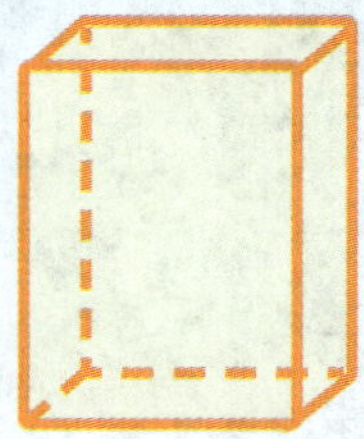

6. Does the solid have any curved surfaces?

Circle: yes no

Directions: Read and solve the problem.

Carrie has 6 shirts and 11 pants. How many shorts does she have if there are 20 pieces of clothing in all?

Draw a picture to show how many shorts Carrie has.

6 + 11 + ☐ = 20

Carrie has ________ shorts.

Directions: Read and solve the problem.

Miguel has 9 crayons and 4 markers. Luz has 7 crayons and 6 markers. They wrote number sentences to show the number of drawing tools they have. Which number sentences are true? Which number sentences are false?

13 = 13	9 – 4 = 7 – 6	9 + 4 = 13
9 + 4 = 7 + 6	13 = 7 + 6	9 + 4 = 7 – 6
9 + 7 = 4 + 6	9 = 13	4 + 9 = 6 + 7

Write each number sentence in the correct place in the chart.

True	False

Directions: Create a map of a town. Use symbols in your map. Write what they stand for in the map key.

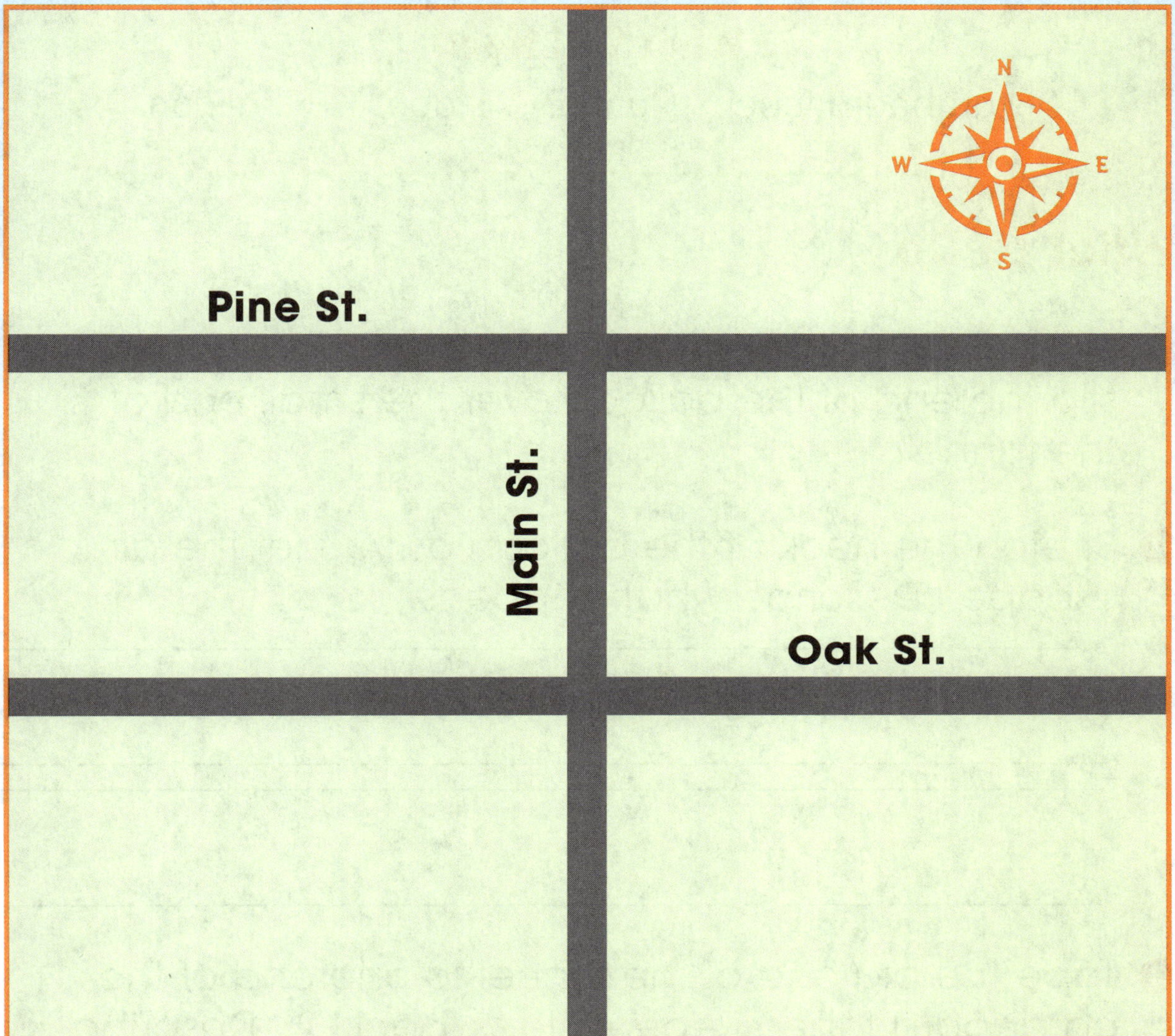

Map Key

Directions: Follow the steps to discover how you can make noise.

What You Need

- cardboard tube
- funnel
- tape
- balloon

What to Do

1. Blow up the balloon. Hold the neck closed, and slip the end of the balloon over the small end of the funnel.

2. Stretch the neck of the balloon as you let the air escape. Describe what happens.

3. Tape the big end of the funnel to one end of the cardboard tube. Repeat steps 1 and 2. Describe what happens.

4. Experiment with different lengths of tube. What changes?

Directions: Place each number below in the puzzle so that the sum of each straight line is 12.

0 1 2 3 4 5 6 7

Directions: Go on a shape scavenger hunt in your house. Try to find each shape shown below. Then, make a map of your house, and draw a picture of each shape in the room where you found it.

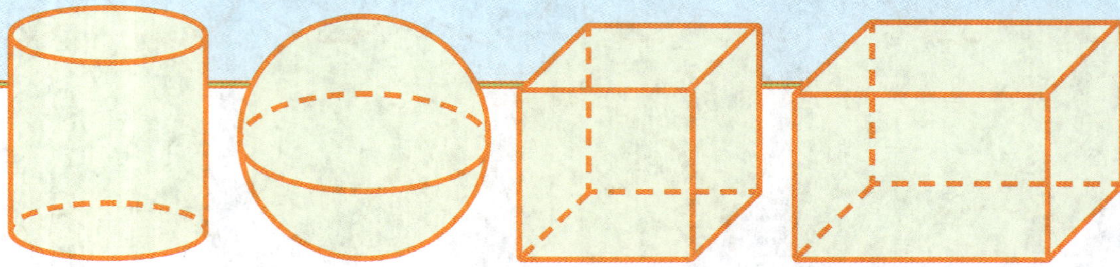

Map Key

High-Frequency Words Activity

Write clues about the high-frequency words from page 129. For example, "This word is a complete thought that begins with a capital letter and ends with a period."

Writing Activity

Talk to an adult about the community worker you wrote about on page 132. Ask him or her what this worker does. Add at least one fact you learned to your writing.

Problem-Solving Activity

Gather 20 counters (crackers, game pieces, cotton balls, etc.). Put them in a brown bag. Take some out of the bag. Figure out how many are still in the bag by counting how many you took out. Repeat several times.

Social Studies Activity

Look at your map from page 137. Explain to a family member which places are near and far from other places on your map.

Critical-Thinking Activity

Explain how you made sums of 12 to solve the puzzle on page 139. Create your own puzzle with sums of 10.

Listening-and-Speaking Activity

Explain to a family member what you discovered in the lab on page 138. Discuss what you could change to get different results.

Directions: Read the text, and answer the questions on the next page.

Nature's Garbage Collector

A turkey vulture is a useful bird. You could call it a garbage collector. It eats meat that other animals leave behind. It will eat all that is left but the bones.

The turkey vulture has a bald head. Its food would stick to the bird's feathers. That bald head helps keep this big bird clean.

A turkey vulture may eat a lot. That can be a problem if a snake wants to eat the vulture for dinner. The bird may be too heavy to fly away. So it does something a bit gross. It throws up some food. Some people think this is so the vulture will get lighter. Others think this is so the snake now has a different dinner. Smart bird!

Directions: Read "Nature's Trash Collector," and then answer the questions.

1. Why would a turkey vulture be called a garbage collector?
   - (A) It eats the bones of animals.
   - (B) It cleans up the mess of other animals.
   - (C) It eats deer and lions.

2. What does the word *bald* mean in this text?
   - (A) without ears
   - (B) without hair
   - (C) without feathers

3. What does a turkey vulture's head look like?
   - (A) black with feathers
   - (B) red and bald
   - (C) brown with one large feather

4. Why does the text say the turkey vulture is a smart bird?
   - (A) It knows how to keep safe from snakes.
   - (B) It knows how to eat meat.
   - (C) It knows how to throw up.

Directions: Read each word. Draw lines between the matching words.

before	right
through	through
right	before
mean	mean
line	too
too	line

Directions: Answer each question.

1. Circle the word that is **not** spelled correctly.

   fast   fist   fost

2. Circle the words that are spelled correctly.

   like   lik   lick

3. Circle the spelling pattern that makes a word that starts with *cl–*.

   –in   –id   –ip

4. Write two words with the *–ake* pattern, as in *cake*.

   ______________   ______________

5. Circle the word that is spelled correctly.

   please   pleez   plese

6. Circle the word that is spelled correctly.

   goeing   gowing   going

Directions: Write the foods you like in each circle. Color the circle with your favorite food. Then, write two reasons why you like that food.

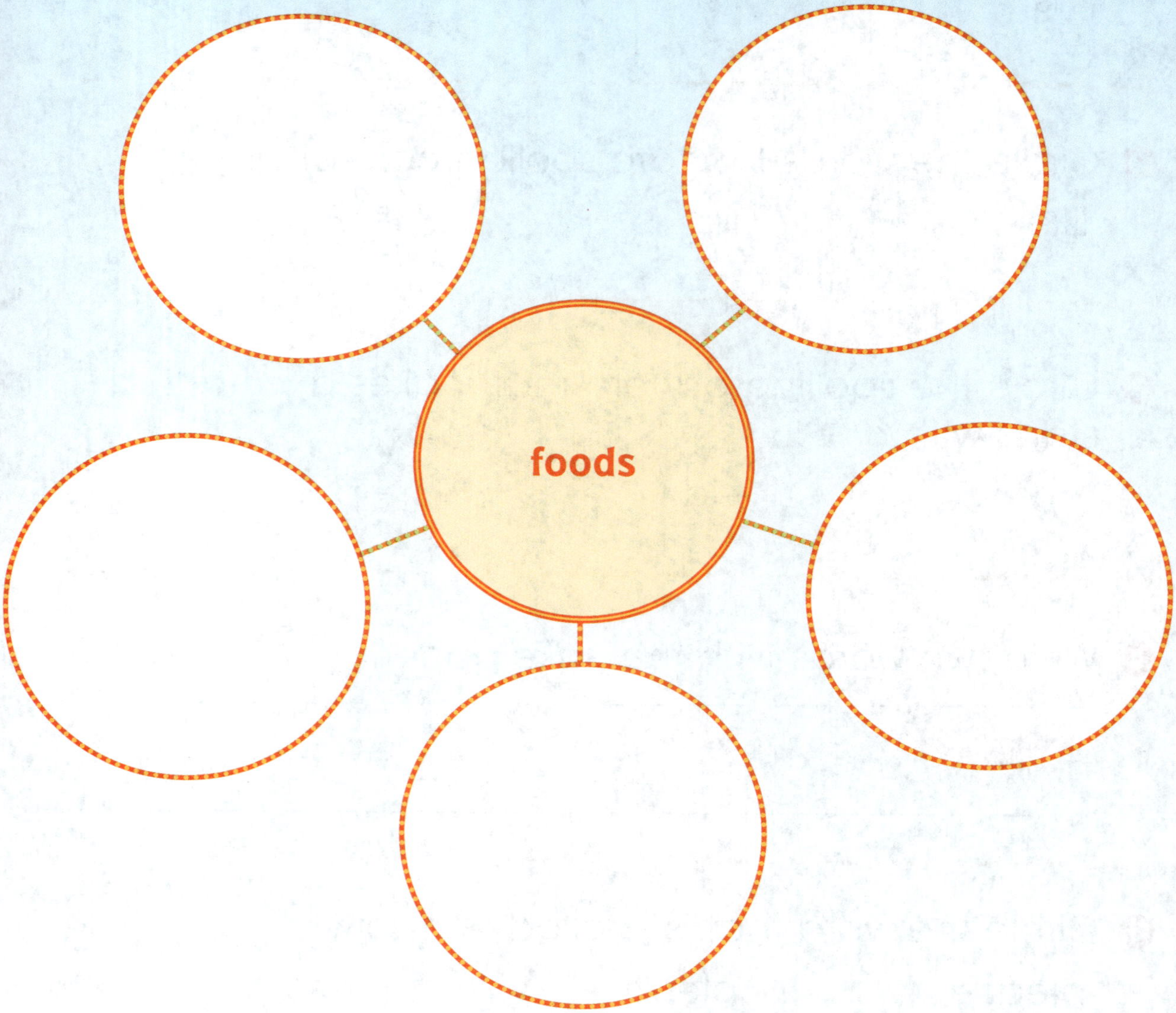

Reason 1

Reason 2

Directions: Draw and write about your favorite food. Include reasons why you like it. Use your notes from page 146 to help you. Then, fill in the checklist.

Opinion

I like ______________________________.

Reasons

____

____

Checklist

- ☐ Sentences begin with capital letters.
- ☐ Sentences end with punctuation.
- ☐ There are spaces between the words.

Directions: Solve each problem.

1. Write the missing numbers.

   ☐ + 4 = 8 8 – ☐ = 4

2. Write the missing numbers.

   9 + 5 = ☐ ☐ – 5 = 9

3. Write the missing subtraction sentence.

   9 + 8 = 17 ☐ – ☐ = ☐

4. Write the missing addition sentence.

   13 – 6 = 7 ☐ + ☐ = ☐

5. Write two different subtraction number sentences with the numbers 3, 5, and 8.

   ______________________ ______________________

6. Write one addition number sentence and one subtraction number sentence with the numbers 1, 6, and 7.

   ______________________ ______________________

Directions: Solve each problem.

1. Write the time.

____ : ____

2. Write the time.

____ : ____

3. Write the time.

____ : ____

4. Write the time.

____ : ____

5. Show 11:00.

6. What are two other ways to write the time twelve thirty?

half past ____

or

____ : ____

Directions: Read and solve the problem.

Which animal is taller, the squirrel or the bird? Use an object to measure each animal.

1. The ______________ is taller.

2. I used a ______________ to measure the animals.

3. The squirrel is ______ ______________ tall.

4. The bird is ______ ______________ tall.

Directions: Draw lines to solve the problem.

Todd wants to cut a triangle into halves and another triangle into fourths.

1. Show how to cut Triangle 1 in half.

Triangle 1

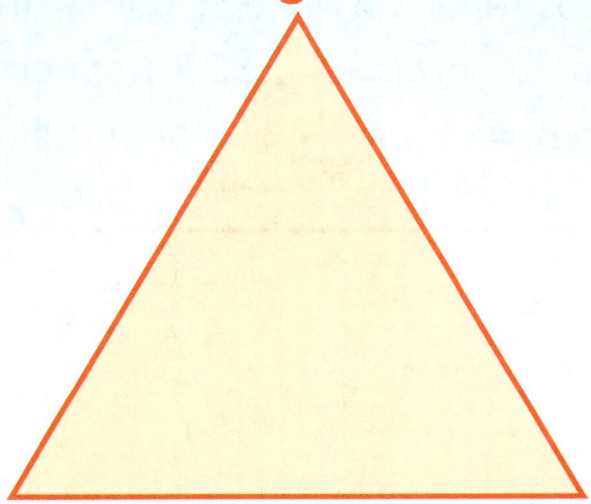

2. Show how to cut Triangle 2 into fourths.

Triangle 2

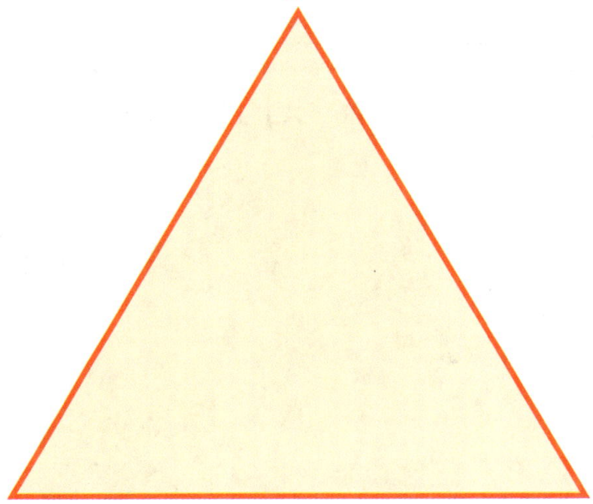

Directions: There are many people in history who made a difference. Circle a person from the list below. Ask an adult to help you learn more about this person. Write and draw what you learned.

Historical People

- Thomas Jefferson
- Abraham Lincoln
- Susan B. Anthony
- Sojourner Truth
- Eleanor Roosevelt
- Martin Luther King Jr.

Draw Picture

Date of Birth: ____________________

Importance

Directions: Follow the steps in the experiment to discover how the sun rises.

What You Need

- table
- flashlight
- sticker
- hand mirror

What to Do

1. Place the sticker on the front of your shirt. You are Earth. The sticker acts like your home.

2. Turn on the flashlight. It acts like the sun. Set it on a desk or table.

3. Turn off the lights. Face the flashlight.

   It is ____________________ at your home.
   (day/night)

4. Turn so your back faces the light.

   It is ____________________ at your home.
   (day/night)

5. Pick up the mirror. It acts like the moon. Light from the sun bounces off the moon. Move the mirror so that the light hits the front of your shirt.

6. Turn to the left until you face the flashlight.

   It is ____________________ at your home.
   (day/night)

Directions: Analogies are words that show relationships. Figure out the relationships between the first pairs of words. Then, write a word for each set that uses the same relationship.

Example: soup : bowl **as** milk : cup.

You put soup in a bowl. You put milk in a cup.

1. legs : walk **as** wings : ____________
2. high : low **as** near : ____________
3. happy : smile **as** sad : ____________
4. pencil : write **as** knife : ____________
5. oak : tree **as** rose : ____________
6. banana : yellow **as** carrot : ____________
7. bed : bedroom **as** oven : ____________
8. doctor : hospital **as** teacher : ____________

Directions: Create a word search using the words in the Word Bank. Write each word in the spaces below. They can go across, down, or diagonal. Then, fill in the rest of the spaces with letters of the alphabet. Challenge another person to find the words you hid.

Word Bank

- vulture
- before
- through
- right
- too
- mean
- line
- time

High-Frequency Words Activity

Write six sentences that each use one of the high-frequency words from page 144.

Mathematics Activity

Create a schedule of your day.

Problem-Solving Activity

Fold a sheet of paper in half. Then, fold it in fourths. How else could you fold it to make equal parts?

Social Studies Activity

Ask an adult to help you research another person from the list on page 152. Create a poster to show how that person helped others.

Critical-Thinking Activity

Write some analogies of your own. Write two related words. Then, write two more words that have the same relationship.

Listening-and-Speaking Activity

Explain to your family what you learned in the lab on page 153. Discuss where the sun and Earth are during the daytime and nighttime.

Answer Key

There are many open-ended pages, problems, and writing prompts in this book. For those activities, the answers will vary. Answers are only given in this answer key if they are specific.

page 7
1. C
2. B
3. B
4. C

page 8
1. B
2. A
3. C
4. C

page 9
1. with
2. they
3. from
4. have
5. are

page 10
1. Sam
2. Any name should be written. The name should be capitalized.
3. Dr. Kim checks teeth.
4. Today's date should be written. The name of the month should be capitalized.
5. Spot

page 13
1. 7
2. 9
3. 7
4. 8
5. 8
6. 7

page 14
1. 3 tens and 7 ones.
2. 45
3. 24
4. 81
5. 16
6. 

page 15

Six more cupcakes should be drawn; 18 cupcakes

page 16

17 toy cars; Student should have drawn 17 toy cars and may have counted the cars by counting on from 10.

page 19

She keeps running away from the ball!

page 20
1. 1 + 30 + 1 + 1 = 33
2. 1 + 1 + 20 + 1 = 23
3. 10 + 1 + 20 = 31
4. 1 + 1 + 40 + 1 = 43
5. 1 + 10 + 1 + 20 = 32
6. from
7. Answers will vary.

page 22
1. B
2. B
3. B
4. C

page 23
1. C
2. B
3. A
4. C

page 24

Words that begin with *w*—was, were, what

Words that have the letter *a*—that, was, what

Words that have three letters—for, was, how

page 25
1. ?
2. !
3. ?
4. .
5. ?
6. !
7. .
8. .

Questions should end in a question mark.

page 28

1. 7
2. 3
3. 4
4. 0
5. 8 – 3 = 5

page 29

1. squares
2. triangles
3. hexagon
4. triangle

page 30

Eleven squares should be drawn with a circle around them; 1 group of ten with 1 left over.

page 31

14 books; 14 books should be drawn with 1 group of ten books circled; 1 ten and 4 ones.

page 32

Possible responses:

Firefighter: hose, ax

Doctor: stethoscope, syringe

Mail Carrier: mailbag, mail truck

Teacher: ruler, books, map

page 37

1. A
2. A
3. C
4. B

page 38

1. B
2. A
3. A
4. C

page 39

1. about
2. use
3. said
4. there
5. two
6. some

page 40

1. bird
2. chair, desk
3. bee
4. tiger
5. dress

page 43

1. 8
2. 6
3. 7
4. 6
5. 8
6. 7
7. 9
8. 8
9. 6
10. 9
11. 7
12. 9

page 44

1. 5
2. 8
3. 6
4. scary
5. cartoon
6. 2

page 45

21 < 31; Cart B has more food items.

page 46

47 of the circles should be colored on the left and 44 circles should be colored on the right; 47 > 44.

page 47

1. service
2. good
3. service
4. good
5. service
6. service
7. good
8. service
9. *good*

page 49

1. ham
2. hat
3. cat
4. mat
5. map
6. mop
7. top
8. stop

page 52

1. B
2. C
3. C
4. A

page 53

1. A
2. C
3. A
4. A

page 54

first	girl	been	their
been	their	write	first
their	would	first	would
write	been	been	girl
girl	their	would	write

page 55

1. went
2. hops
3. moved
4. means
5. found

page 58

1. 5
2. 1
3. 0
4. 2
5. 4
6. 6
7. 4
8. 6
9. 1
10. 2
11. 1
12. 3

page 59

1. 71
2. 58
3. 49
4. 36, 38
5. 80, 88, 91
6. 32, 29, 21

page 60

Nine more circles in the ten frames;
$8 + 9 = 17$; $17 - 8 = 9$

page 61

Student may have colored 20 circles in the 2 ten frames and crossed out 9 circles; $9 + 11 = 20$; $20 - 9 = 11$; 11 books
Challenge: 16 books

page 64

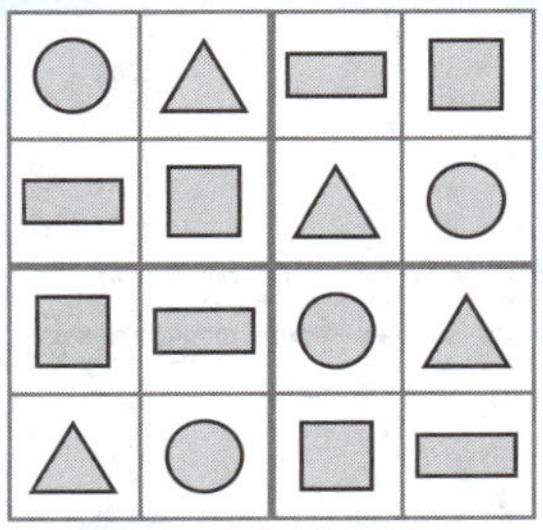

3	1	4	2
2	4	3	1
1	3	2	4
4	2	1	3

page 67

1. C
2. A
3. A
4. B

page 68

1. C
2. B
3. A
4. A

page 69

1. wood
2. train
3. gum
4. pay
5. cut
6. shoe

page 70

1. I
2. me
3. she
4. Any pronoun that makes sense such as: We, They, He, or She
5. We

page 73

1. 12
2. 10
3. 12
4. 15
5. 13
6. 14
7. 10
8. 13
9. 14
10. 17
11. 15
12. 18

page 74

1. yes
2. 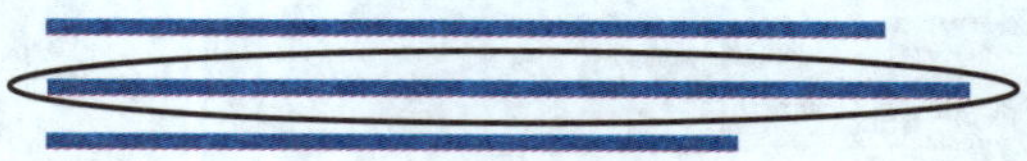
3. 4 paper clips
4. 2 clothespins
5. 7 squares

page 75

The hundreds chart should show 45 blue squares and 12 red squares in some way; Kate has 57 shells now.

page 76

65 girls are on the swim team; 10 girls join the team; Student may have counted the girls by counting 10 more from 65, or moved down one row on the hundreds chart; 75 girls are on the team now.

page 83

1. B
2. B
3. B
4. C

page 84

1. little
2. over
3. know
4. sound
5. Only
6. take

page 85

1. come
2. every, walk
3. here
4. Accept any real word with the *–ill* pattern. Examples: *dill, fill, gill, hill, Jill, kill, mill, pill, sill, will.*
5. your
6. there

page 88

1. 5
2. 3
3. 10
4. 8
5. 1
6. 16
7. 15
8. 11
9. 12
10. 7
11. 5
12. 1

page 89

1. 14
2. 12
3. 10
4. 13
5. 18
6. 17
7. 14
8. 11
9. 16
10. 11
11. 13
12. 14

page 90

1. Student should have completed the chart by writing 4 tally marks for green, 4 tally marks for red, and 7 tally marks for blue.
2. 3 friends
3. 15 friends

page 91

Possible answers:

1.

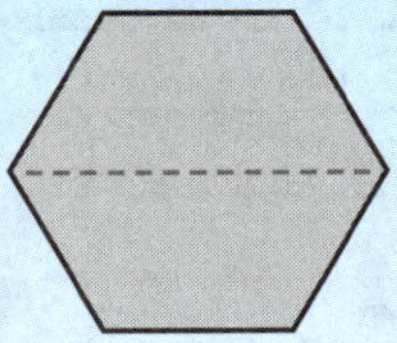

2.

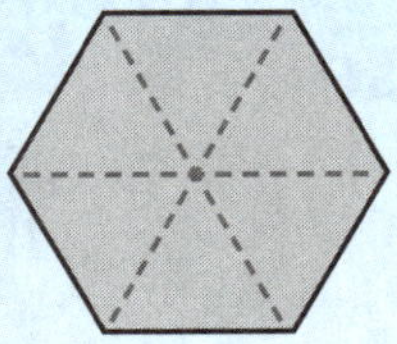

page 94

1. young or new
2. strong
3. wide
4. smooth
5. light
6. easy
7. cheap
8. deep
9. wealthy or rich
10. loose

page 98

1. A
2. B
3. B
4. A

page 99

1. after
2. very
3. live
4. back
5. work

page 100

1. girls
2. car
3. snakes
4. Bananas
5. boy
6. dogs

page 103

1. true
2. 4 + 4, 10 – 2, 12 – 4
3. –
4. +
5. 2
6. 5 + 5, 2+ 8, 13 – 3
7. 2
8. –

page 104

1. >
2. =
3. <
4. 38
5. Any number less than 58.
6. Any number greater than 44.

page 105

Possible answers: 2 tens and 5 ones; 1 ten and 15 ones; 0 tens and 25 ones.

page 106

Example:

Shorter than my foot	Same length as my foot	Longer than my foot
eraser	book	door
crayon	pencil	flag
cube	paper	jump rope

page 107

Wants: TV, toys, games, bike

Needs: water, food, clothes, place to live

page 109

1. a sad dad
2. a fat cat
3. a rich witch
4. a flat hat
5. a pig wig

page 113

1. A
2. B
3. B
4. B

page 115

1. red
2. pretty
3. Any adjective that describes a song such as: pretty, loud, or sad.
4. Any two adjectives that describe a flower.
5. Any two adjectives that describe a sweater.

page 118

1. 4
2. 5
3. 4
4. 4
5. 1
6. 2
7. 6
8. 7
9. 10
10. 12
11. 0
12. 3

page 119

1. 5
2. strawberry
3. chocolate
4. 3
5. 8
6. 14

page 120

14 pens; Student may have drawn a picture to show a total of 17 pens with 3 pens crossed out or may have written the equations $6 + 7 + 4 = 17$ and $17 - 3 = 14$.

page 121

70 books; Student should have colored 90 circles in the ten frames and crossed out 2 complete ten frames.

page 122

Possible Answers:

1. picture of a computer and keyboard, pen, pencil
2. picture of a washing machine
3. picture of a cell phone
4. picture of a car or bus

page 124

	Apple	Pineapple	Banana	Pear
Pete				✓
Jamal			✓	
Raj	✓			
Pearl		✓		

page 128

1. A
2. B
3. C
4. A

page 129

1. kh**think**tni
2. ysya**say**asy
3. t**sentence**n
4. erhr**where**w
5. pleh**help**el
6. **much**cumchu

page 130

1. saying
2. helped
3. walks, walking
4. works, worked, working

page 133

1. 7
2. 2
3. 11
4. 9
5. 8
6. 4
7. 7
8. 14
9. 5
10. 7
11. 11
12. 16

page 134

1. Any of these lines may be drawn:

2. The rectangle should be circled.
3. yes
4. The number cube should be circled.
5. The box of soap should be circled.
6. yes

page 135

6 + 11 + 3 = 20; Carrie has 3 shorts.

page 136

True	False
13 = 13	9 + 7 = 4 + 6
9 + 4 = 7 + 6	9 − 4 = 7 − 6
13 = 7 + 6	9 = 13
9 + 4 = 13	9 + 4 = 7 − 6
4 + 9 = 6 + 7	

page 139

Example:

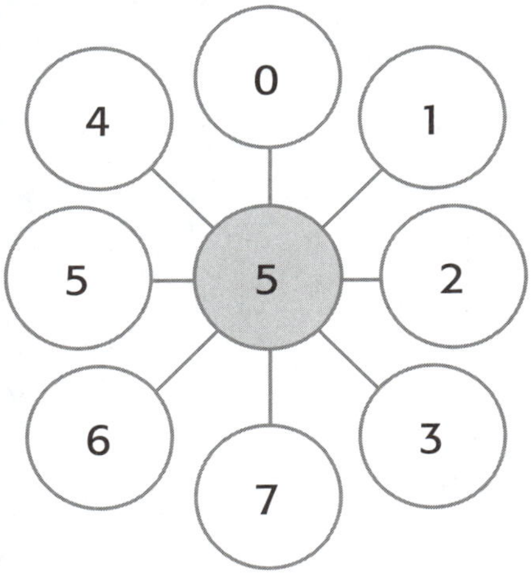

page 143

1. B
2. C
3. B
4. A

page 144

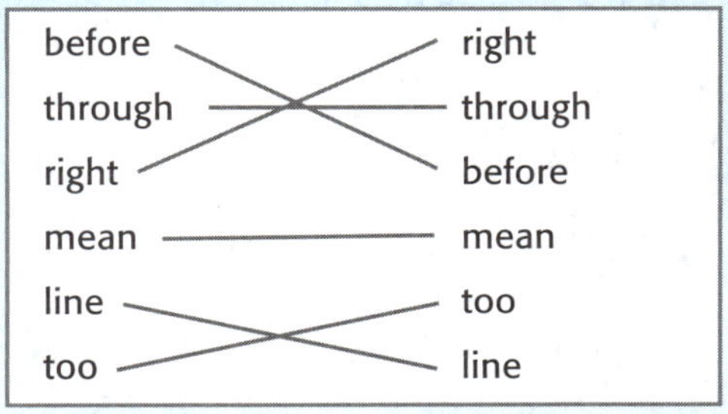

page 145

1. fost
2. like, lick
3. *–ip*
4. Accept any real words with the *–ake* pattern. Example: *bake, fake, lake, make, rake, take, wake.*
5. please
6. going

page 148

1. 4, 4
2. 14, 14
3. 17 − 9 = 8 or 17 − 8 = 9
4. 6 + 7 = 13 or 7 + 6 = 13
5. 8 − 5 = 3 and 8 − 3 = 5
6. 1 + 6 = 7 or 6 + 1 = 7 and 7 − 1 = 6 or 7 − 6 = 1

page 149

1. 10:00
2. 10:30
3. 1:00
4. 6:30
5.

6. half past 12 or 12:30

page 150

1. The squirrel is taller.
2. Possible answers:
   I used a paper clip to measure the animals.
3. Possible answers:
   The squirrel is 2 paper clips tall.
4. Possible answers:
   The bird is 1 paper clip tall.

page 151

Possible answers:

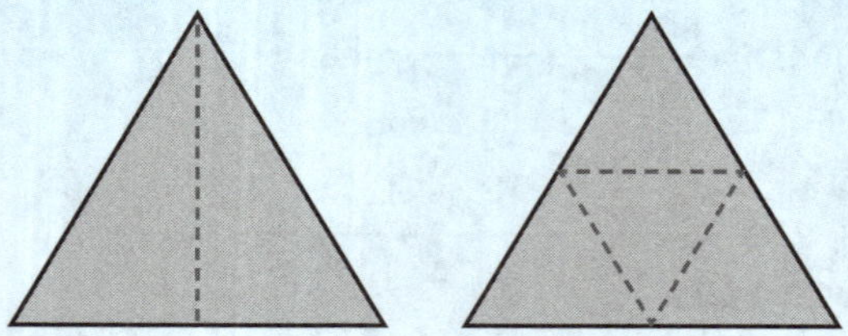

page 153

3. day
4. night
6. day

page 154

1. fly
2. far
3. frown
4. cut
5. flower
6. orange
7. kitchen
8. school

Skills and Standards in This Book

Today's standards have created more consistency in how they mathematics and English language arts are taught. In the past, states and school districts had their own standards for each grade level. However, what was taught at a specific grade in one location may have been taught at a different grade in another location. This made it difficult when students moved.

Today, many states and school districts have adopted new standards. This means that for the first time, there is greater consistency in what is being taught at each grade level, with the ultimate goal of getting students ready to be successful in college and in their careers.

Standards Features

The overall goal for the standards is to better prepare students for life. Today's standards have several key features:

- They describe what students should know and be able to do at each grade level.
- They are rigorous and dive deeply into the content.
- They require higher-level thinking and analysis.
- They require students to explain and justify answers.
- They are aimed at making sure students are prepared for college and/or their future careers.

Unit Outline

This book is designed to help your child meet today's rigorous standards. This section describes the standards-based skills covered in each unit of study.

Unit 1	• Read and answer questions about a narrative and a piece of nonfiction text. • Practice reading and writing high-frequency words. • Use correct capitalization. • Write an opinion about an animal.	• Use strategies to add within 20. • Understand place value. • Use map keys. • Identify patterns in sunrise and sunset times.
Unit 2	• Read and answer questions about a narrative and a piece of nonfiction text. • Practice reading and writing high-frequency words. • Use correct punctuation. • Write a narrative about playing with a friend. • Subtract within 10.	• Identify shapes that compose a larger shape. • Understand place value. • Identify types of community workers. • Observe plants in the local environment.
Unit 3	• Read and answer questions about a narrative and a piece of nonfiction text. • Practice reading and writing high-frequency words. • Identify and write nouns. • Write an informative text about a flag.	• Add within 10. • Interpret charts. • Use models to compare numbers. • Identify goods and services. • Observe the effects of heat and sunlight.
Unit 4	• Read and answer questions about a narrative and a piece of nonfiction text. • Practice reading high-frequency words. • Identify and write verbs. • Write an opinion about a holiday.	• Add and subtract within 20. • Place numbers in ascending and descending order. • Create a time line. • Observe the lunar phases.
Unit 5	• Read and answer questions about a narrative and a piece of nonfiction text. • Practice reading high-frequency words. • Identify and write pronouns. • Write a narrative about a vacation. • Add within 20.	• Measure the lengths of objects. • Use strategies to add numbers. • Identify the purpose of rules. • Identify how baby animals resemble their parents.

Unit 6	• Read and answer questions about a piece of nonfiction text. • Practice reading and writing high-frequency words. • Use conventional spelling for words with common spelling. • Write an informative text about a bird.	• Add and subtract within 20. • Create and interpret charts. • Identify shapes that compose a larger shape. • Vote on a family game. • Observe the connection between sounds and vibrations.
Unit 7	• Read and answer questions about a narrative. • Practice reading and writing high-frequency words. • Identify and write nouns. • Write an opinion about a sport.	• Add and subtract within 20. • Use place value to compare numbers. • Find the relative lengths of objects. • Identify wants and needs. • Create a model to show Earth and the moon move.
Unit 8	• Read and answer questions about a piece of nonfiction text. • Practice reading and writing high-frequency words. • Identify and write adjectives. • Write a narrative about a trip.	• Add and subtract within 20. • Interpret data into a chart. • Use strategies to add and subtract. • Identify how things change over time. • Observe plants growing from seeds.
Unit 9	• Read and answer questions about a narrative. • Practice reading high-frequency words. • Use correct verb tenses. • Write an informative text about community workers.	• Add and subtract within 20. • Identify solid shapes. • Use strategies to add and subtract. • Create a town map. • Experiment with how to amplify sounds.
Unit 10	• Read and answer questions about a piece of nonfiction text. • Practice reading and writing high-frequency words. • Use conventional spelling for words with common spelling. • Write an opinion about food. • Add and subtract within 20.	• Write and tell time to the nearest half hour. • Measure the lengths of objects. • Cut shapes into equal parts. • Research a historical figure. • Create a model to show why the sun appears to rise and set.

Congratulations

______________________________!

(name)

You have completed
Conquering First Grade!

presented on ____________________
(date)